TIPPECANOE COUNTY AND THE 1913 FLOOD

TIPPECANOE COUNTY AND THE 1913 FLOOD

PETE BILL & ARNOLD L. SWEET

THE History PRESS

Published by The History Press
Charleston, SC
www.historypress.com

First published 2021

Manufactured in the United States

ISBN 9781467147583

Library of Congress Control Number: 2020951819

Notice: The information in this book is true and complete to the best of our knowledge. It is offered without guarantee on the part of the authors or The History Press. The authors and The History Press disclaim all liability in connection with the use of this book.

Thanks to my wife, Lorita, for supporting the production of this book.
—Pete Bill

In remembrance of Janet Ailsa Rae Sweet, who put up with my postcard collecting. Also, thank you to the members of the Indianapolis Postcard Club. If not for them, I would not have collected the postcards that are used in this book.
—Arnold L. Sweet

CONTENTS

ACKNOWLEDGEMENTS

Special thanks to the dedicated staff and volunteers at the Tippecanoe County Historical Association of Lafayette, Indiana, for contributing advice and several rare images to this publication.

INTRODUCTION

The 1913 flood and the disruptive March weather with which it was affiliated made headlines in almost every state in the United States. Large metropolitan areas like Indianapolis and Dayton, Ohio, had strong news-gathering centers that were capable of documenting their particular views of the disaster and disseminating them across the telegraph wires to all corners of the continent. Other, smaller communities with less access to communication still had their stories told because their particular twists on the disaster made for good newsprint. For example, the circus animals that were lost in the flood in Peru, Indiana, and the flood-threatened orphanage at Fort Wayne, Indiana, both figured prominently in stories published in 1913 and in the flood centennial publications of 2013.

However, the devastating weather in March 1913 also produced thousands of other stories that were not newsworthy enough to be selected for publication in prominent newspapers or chosen by authors for inclusion in the books written in 1913 and 1914 about the 1913 flood. Since 1913, there have been many other floods and disasters, and with the advent of increasingly sophisticated means with which to broadcast news in ways that better capture the public's attention, the events of 1913 have largely been forgotten by the citizens of the same communities that were devastated—that is, until a centennial or other anniversary occurs. This is especially true in the smaller communities that were hit equally as hard as the more publicized communities but whose stories were told only in local small-circulation newspapers or journals.

This book seeks to help preserve some of the stories of the 1913 weather disaster that affected the citizens of Tippecanoe County and the surrounding area. The individual stories are no less heroic or tragic than the more widely publicized events, but they are largely unknown and have been overshadowed and forgotten. Even within Indiana today, historical presentations of the Great Flood of 1913 by state organizations rarely give but a passing reference to any of the stories of Tippecanoe County. The 1913 book by Logan Marshall titled *The True Story of Our National Calamity of Flood, Fire, and Tornado* devoted three paragraphs of its 320 pages to Tippecanoe County. The more recent 2013 publication, *Washed Away* by Geoff Williams, focuses largely on Fort Wayne, Peru and Indianapolis in Indiana, although it does devote 6 pages of one section specifically to Lafayette, Indiana.

The oversight of Tippecanoe County in the 1913 disaster is neither malicious nor historical malpractice but simply reflects that the story of the March 1913 flood, tornadoes and their subsequent destruction provides sufficient fodder to fill many volumes of books with tales of tragedy or survival. Thus, this book is intended to capture the stories of one often-overlooked area affected by the 1913 weather disaster: Tippecanoe County, Indiana.

The 1913 flood is relatively well documented, with far more images from amateur photographers than floods and other disasters would have had only a few years before. Many of the photographs included in this book are referred to as "real photograph postcards," or RPPC, because a "real" photograph, taken either by amateurs or professionals, could have been printed on one side of a postcard and a format for an address and sometimes a message could have been printed on the other. By 1913, the presence of real photograph postcards was well established in U.S. culture. In 1903, Kodak introduced the concept of RPPC with a small folding pocket camera that captured images on a postcard-sized negative (three and a half inches by five and a half inches). These phtographs could then be transferred onto postcard paper stock for mailing through the U.S. Postal Service. By 1907, Kodak capitalized on the popularity of RPPCs by providing a service that would turn any sized picture taken on any camera brand into an RPPC. The availability of affordable cameras, plus the popularity of "publishing" personal photographs for friends and family members, meant that hundreds of photographers were available in 1913 to document the events surrounding the 1913 storms and flood across the affected states. Some cameras during this time had a small opening on the back that allowed photographers to scratch in a short description, such as a date, location or their name.[1] Several of the photographs in this book are from RPPCs that have such markings.

One contributor whose signature is found on several RPPCs in this book was Dr. William Marven Reser. Dr. Reser was a physician who was born and raised in Tippecanoe County; he practiced medicine in Lafayette and donated his services to the county's orphanage for twenty-five years. He was an avid photographer and enthusiastic historian, recording images from all around Tippecanoe County throughout his life. He wrote extensively about the Wabash and Erie Canal and many other historical events and features of the county. He served as president of the Tippecanoe County Historical Association (TCHA), and after his passing, he donated many manuscripts, photographs and items of historical significance to TCHA and the Indiana Historical Society. We are fortunate to have a number of postcards and RPPCs either taken or collected by William M. Reser included in this book.

Because many of the images in this book came from amateur photographers like Dr. Reser, local events, including the 1913 flood, were captured as they unfolded. As such, many of the images in this book are being published in a text for the first time. We are very thankful for the dozens of amateur photographers who chose to document events of the 1913 flood, freezing the images in time with their own personal cameras and printing their photographs on the sturdy postcard stock that survived for over one hundred years.

Chapter 1

LAFAYETTE, WEST LAFAYETTE AND TIPPECANOE COUNTY IN 1913

The city of Lafayette and the surrounding Tippecanoe County have changed considerably from the thickly covered tracts of plum bushes, hazel brush, wild grapevines and dense wood that were purchased by William Digby at a federal government land sale held in Crawfordsville, Indiana, on December 24, 1824, for the sum of $231.63.[2] Being the farthest town upstream on the navigable portion of the Wabash River from Vincennes made Lafayette a natural jumping-off point for trade of goods to this part of west-central Indiana. The completion of the Wabash and Erie Canal to Lafayette from the northeast in 1843 allowed commerce to travel upstream and downstream from Lafayette and connected Tippecanoe County to goods and services originating from Ohio and points to the east. Before long, the railroads supplanted the canal system, and Tippecanoe County became a crossroads of rail traffic, with five railroads running through the county, four of which intersected in Lafayette.[3]

Industry in Lafayette flourished in the late nineteenth century, and in 1891, forward-thinking city fathers implemented a belt-railway to give Lafayette factories on the city's east side better access to the main rail lines for distributing their manufactured goods across the continent.[4] Electric railway systems—the interurban—sprang up, connecting rural parts of Tippecanoe County and other parts of Indiana to Lafayette and its adjoining communities, and they allowed easy transport of people to and from work in the city.

To supply the rapidly growing community, power and water had to be readily available. In the 1909 publication *Past and Present of Tippecanoe County, Indiana*, the writers lauded the water supply for Lafayette as being "one of the purest, most health-giving waters found in use in any of the cities of this country."[5] A system of forty-six six-inch wells was sunk to thirty-five feet below the riverbed of the Wabash in sand and gravel, allowing for natural filtration of any surface water that might seep downward into the aquifer. A pumping station along the river pushed the filtered water up the eastern Wabash River escarpment to the Columbian Park Reservoir, which, being elevated above the city, provided the water pressure needed for tap water and fire hydrants used in the city below. Likewise, West Lafayette had a pumping house and accompanying boiler house built for $5,500 that was put into operation on February 7, 1894. The pumps tapped into eleven wells located on the western bank of the Wabash River and pulled water from between sixty-five and eighty feet below ground level, ensuring that surface water would not contaminate the deep-water supply. Water from the West Lafayette wells was pumped to a large steel tank that was located two hundred feet above the river at the top of the hill at the corner of what is today Salisbury and Grant Streets.[6] It's important to note that both pumping stations were dependent on fire-heated boilers to drive the steam pumps necessary to push the water to either the standing steel tank for West Lafayette or the Columbian Park Reservoir, which, in turn, supplied the necessary water pressure to deliver water to hydrants and household faucets.

Electricity came to Lafayette in 1884, and in 1888, the Citizen's Natural Gas Company piped natural gas from the eastern Indiana gas fields to heat and light the homes and factories in Lafayette. When the natural gas sources in the eastern Indiana gas fields became depleted at the end of the nineteenth century, the illuminating gas used in Lafayette was manufactured by burning coal. The large gasworks plant in Lafayette supplied gas not only to Lafayette but also to West Lafayette, passing along gas lines that extended across the Wabash River under the decking of the Main Street Bridge.[7] In 1908, the Merchants Electric Light Association built a larger electricity-generating plant near the Wabash River at the foot of Cincinnati Street and used coal-burning, steam-powered dynamos to produce enough electricity and hot water to supply the entire city. By 1913, electricity was being generated by more than one location, with the Indiana Lighting Company's plant located on Fourth Street, 356 feet from the foot of the Brown Street Bridge and near the Merchants Electric Light Association Plant. Additional electricity was generated from the power plants that were owned by electric streetcar

Columbian Park Reservoir pumping station, circa 1910. The Lafayette waterworks pulled water from its deep-driven wells near the Wabash River. Steam-driven pumps pushed the water two hundred feet vertically up the eastern river escarpment to the Columbian Park Reservoir. The Columbian Park Reservoir pumping station supplied water pressure to homes along the eastern escarpment and pushed water through pipes back to downtown Lafayette. *From the collection of Pete Bill.*

companies like the Fort Wayne and Northern Indiana Traction Company, and they provided additional but far smaller amounts of electricity to the community. Like the gas generated by Lafayette, the electricity generated by Lafayette powerhouses also supplied the West Lafayette community, primarily via electrical lines across the Brown Street, Main Street and, to a lesser degree, the Big Four/New York Central System Railroad Bridges.

Bridges: The Transportation Arteries for Tippecanoe County

Even more so than today, in 1913, the bridges in Tippecanoe County were vital connections between the opposite sides of the Wabash River. Because many students, university employees and West Lafayette business and factory workers actually lived in Lafayette, the bridges were essential for allowing efficient transport of these people daily between their jobs and homes. Livestock, manufactured goods and products also moved back and forth, linking the manufacturing and agricultural economies of the communities on either side of the river. Although ferries were employed in areas with less demand for constant travel across the Wabash River, the bridges were essential for the higher volume of people, livestock and goods that had to be moved across the river.

The first bridge across the Wabash River that connected Lafayette and what would become West Lafayette was a wooden-planked structure that was constructed in 1847 as a result of a stock company being formed in 1845 by businessmen John Purdue, Nathan H. Stockwell, John L. Reynolds, Robert Heath and David Ross. The wooden bridge was located at Brown Street and provided a faster and easier way for people, wagons and livestock to get across the river, and it was likely viewed by the invested businessmen as a way to increase profitable traffic to support their respective businesses. Because Lafayette was the farthest town upstream on navigable Wabash River headwater in the mid-1800s, bridges had to accommodate the larger Mississippi steamboats by incorporating a center "draw" section of the wooden bridge. For those traveling over the bridge, the bridge was a toll bridge that charged fares of fifty cents for four-horse wagon teams, twenty-five cents for two-horse wagons, twenty cents for buggies and six and one-quarter cents for foot passengers, cattle and horses. Pigs and sheep were charged the relative bargain price of three cents per head.[8] The solid stone piers on which the sturdy Brown Street Bridge wooden structure had been built withstood the significant Wabash River floods in August 1878 and the worst recorded flood (prior to 1913) of February 17, 1883.

With the success of the first bridge at Brown Street, the same group of investors had a second wooden bridge erected in 1863 that connected the Main Streets on both sides of the Wabash River. Like the first bridge—and similar to many of the privately owned roadways of the time—this wooden bridge was also a toll bridge. Both bridges remained toll bridges until 1875, when the county purchased both bridges and removed the toll. The wooden Main Street Bridge was replaced with a state-of-the-art steel bridge in 1889; it was constructed by the Lafayette Bridge Company under the supervision of civil engineer Everett B. Vawter. Its cost was double that of the wooden structure, but it had a wider roadway that was covered with brick and cement. To accommodate greater traffic, in 1895, a separate electric streetcar track for the Fort Wayne and Wabash Valley Traction Company (later reorganized into the Fort Wayne and Northern Indiana Traction Company in 1911 and referred to in this book by that name) was built on the north side of the Main Street Bridge by extending the bridge deck, and a separate pedestrian

An artist's depiction of the Main Street Bridge around 1890 but before 1895. The large stone piers on which the elaborate steelwork spans sat were later widened in 1912 to better support the electric streetcar track. This pier widening would play a role in the problems that occurred with the bridge during the 1913 flood. *From the collection of Pete Bill.*

walkway was built on the south side of the bridge.[9] With its modern and somewhat elaborate ironwork, the Main Street Bridge soon became the most heavily traveled bridge in the county.

The sturdy, wooden, covered Brown Street Bridge served its purpose until Sunday, October 6, 1901, when a fire, either set deliberately or accidentally by one of the electrical wires that was carried by the bridge, was spied burning the fifty-four-year-old weathered and dried timbers at about 1:30 a.m. The fire did extensive damage, and the $5,000 worth of insurance on the structure was deemed insufficient to repair it. The decision was made to demolish the rest of the wooden structure and to erect a modern steel-truss bridge set on the same sturdy stone piers that the wooden structure had been set on. The modern design of the Brown Street Bridge included an asphalt roadway, which was considered new and innovative at the time. Because the Wabash and Erie Canal had fallen into disuse several years prior, it had been filled in on the eastern approach to new Brown Street Bridge, allowing the bridge to be shorter than the original wood bridge that had to span both the Wabash River and the canal. In 1902, the modern steel-truss Brown Street Bridge was completed. Owing to its construction and the apparent strength

The Main Street Bridge supported automobile and wagon traffic and the Fort Wayne and Northern Indiana Traction Company's electric streetcar track. Electrical wires ran along the top of the bridge to power the streetcars and carry electricity, and telephone wires ran overhead and below the bridge decking to provide phone service to West Lafayette. Gas lines were carried under the bridge decking. *From the postcard collection of Arnold L. Sweet.*

of the stone piers built in 1847, the bridge withstood the March 15, 1907 flood with no apparent damage to its piers or structure.[10]

The third bridge across the Wabash River in downtown Lafayette was the bridge over which the Big Four (Cleveland, Cincinnati, Chicago and St. Louis Railway, abbreviated "CCCStL") and the Lake Erie and Western Railroads ran. Both railways were part of the extensive New York Central System; therefore, the railroad bridge in Lafayette was often referred to as the New York Central Bridge or the Big Four Bridge. Although a rail bridge existed across the Wabash at this same site before 1906, the more modern version of the railroad bridge was built on wide stone piers in 1906. To ensure a gentler downward slope of the railroad bed as it came off the elevated western escarpment and headed across the Wabash to Lafayette, a large amount of earth was moved into the Chauncey Bottomlands south of Main Street near the Detention Hospital to build up an embankment for the tracks. At the time of the flood in 1913, the two sets of tracks across the Wabash constituted a major artery for goods and people traveling on the Lake Erie and Western Line to and from the eastern part of Indiana and mid-central Illinois or connecting Indianapolis and Chicago via the Big Four tracks.

The New York Central System's railroad bridge (circa 1910) carried tracks for the Cleveland, Cincinnati, Chicago and St. Louis Railroad (the "Big Four") and the Lake Erie & Western Railroad. *From the postcard collection of Arnold L. Sweet.*

The New York Central System's railroad bridge, as viewed from the West Lafayette side, showing the two sets of tracks. The dome of the Tippecanoe County Courthouse can be seen jutting above the downtown Lafayette skyline. *From the postcard collection of Arnold L. Sweet.*

As mentioned previously, in addition to transporting people, livestock and goods via rail across the river, basic utilities and communication lines for the citizens, businesses and homes in West Lafayette were carried across the bridges from Lafayette generating plants. The gas production plant and the major electricity power plants were all located near the Brown Street Bridge, and hence, early on, the Brown Street Bridge provided a major umbilical artery for utilities during the town's early years. The burning of the Brown Street Bridge in 1901 interrupted electricity for lighting and telephone communication to the river's west side for days. With the development of the more modern Main Street Bridge, more electrical lines, gas pipelines, telephone and telegraph lines were shifted from the Brown Street Bridge and suspended across that Main Street Bridge. It would not be an exaggeration to say that, in 1913, normal life in Lafayette and West Lafayette was dependent on intact and functional bridges.

Lafayette as seen from Union Street and North Fourth Street, overlooking the Indiana Lighting Company. This photograph and was probably taken from the Thieme and Wagner Brewing Company. The Brown Street and Main Street bridges and the railroad bridge can be seen in succession from closest to farthest. *From the postcard collection of Arnold L. Sweet.*

The steel bridges that were built across the Wabash River between 1890 and 1912 were vital lifelines for the county. This photograph shows the 1912 construction of the Jewettsport Ford Bridge north of Lafayette and just outside of Battleground. This bridge survived the 1913 flood, was rehabilitated in 1989 and still carries one-lane automobile traffic between Battleground and old State Road 25. *From the postcard collection of Arnold L. Sweet.*

TIPPECANOE COUNTY'S DEPENDENCE ON RAIL

In spite of its promise as a means for efficient transportation of goods across Indiana, the Wabash and Erie Canal, which opened in 1841, had largely been abandoned by the 1870s. By the end of the nineteenth century, neglect had allowed the canal to become a shallow, stagnant eyesore, with many segments being filled in with dirt. Indeed, during an 1885 visit to Lafayette, Mark Twain, the noted humorist and author, remarked dryly, "You have a very fine city here. I particularly admire your grand canal."[11] By 1913, many of the east–west-oriented city roads, like Cincinnati Street, North Street, Columbia Street and South Street, traveled over the filled, shallow remnants of the canal and terminated on the other side of the canal at the banks of the Wabash River.

The demise of the Wabash and Erie Canal was primarily due to the proliferation of steam rail services that more effectively connected Lafayette and Tippecanoe County to all points in Indiana and the country beyond. Lafayette's location on a straight line between Indianapolis and Chicago, and on a line between eastern Indiana cities and Chicago and Peoria, Illinois, made it an ideal junction point for several steam locomotive railroad lines carrying passengers and freight.

The previously mentioned Cleveland, Cincinnati, Chicago and St. Louis Railway, or Big Four Railroad, brought freight and passengers into Lafayette from Indianapolis via the southwest corner of the county, passing through Lebanon, Thorntown, Colfax and Clarks Hill along the way. The Big Four Line crossed the Wabash River over the double-tracked New York Central System railroad bridge alongside the Lake Erie and Western Track, then continued northwest, parallel to what is now State Road 52, to the small town of Templeton. At Templeton, the Big Four split from the shared track of the Lake Erie and Western Railway and continued northwest to Kankakee, Illinois, eventually turning north to transport cargo to Chicago.

The second major steam locomotive rail line through Tippecanoe County was the Lake Erie and Western Railroad (LEW), which, like the Big Four Railway, was also part of the New York Central System. The Lake Erie and Western brought rail traffic westward from Muncie, Indiana, via Tipton and through Frankfort. After entering Tippecanoe County, the LEW shared trackage with the Big Four Railroad through Lafayette and across the Wabash River via the Big Four/New York Central System Bridge. After crossing the river, the two New York Central System lines shared track northwestward to Templeton, where the Lake Erie and Western split from the Big Four to head due west to serve mid-central Illinois cities.

The third major set of tracks in Tippecanoe County belonged to the Chicago, Indianapolis and Louisville Railway, known today as the Monon. It was the first railway through Lafayette and was completed in the autumn of 1852 as the New Albany and Salem Railroad (it was renamed a few years later the Louisville, New Albany and Chicago Railway). This line carried rail traffic between New Albany, Indiana, and Louisville, Kentucky, on the Ohio River all the way to Chicago. Locally, the Monon tracks ran due north from Crawfordsville, through Linden and Romney and into downtown Lafayette. Until 1994, the Monon ran directly through downtown Lafayette and stopped at a depot located on Fifth Street. From downtown, the rails coursed northeastward and crossed the Wabash River north of Lafayette, near Davis Ferry and the location of today's North Ninth Street Bridge. The Monon tracks entered the town of Battleground, then turned north, continuing parallel to what is now State Road 43, passing through Brookston until it reached its namesake town of Monon, where the track split into two tracks, serving Chicago and Michigan City.[12]

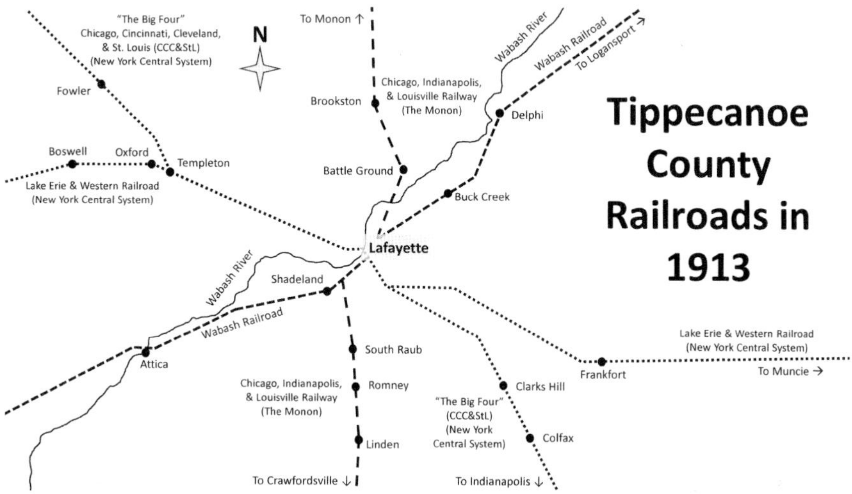

In 1913, Lafayette was at the confluence of four major railways: the Monon, the Big Four, the Wabash and the Lake Erie and Western. These railroads shifted Lafayette's mode of transportation of goods from the river and Erie Canal to rail. Electric interurban railcars from the Terre Haute, Indianapolis and Eastern and the Fort Wayne and Northern Indiana Traction companies carried people between Lafayette and communities to the south and east daily. *Map constructed by authors.*

Finally, the fourth steam rail to pass through Lafayette was the legendary Wabash Railroad, to which the popular early twentieth-century American folksong "The Wabash Cannonball" is attributed. The Wabash Railroad brought rail traffic into Lafayette from Fort Wayne and northeast Indiana via the towns of Wabash, Peru and Logansport. The Wabash Railroad crossed into Tippecanoe County, passing over Wildcat Creek north of Lafayette, near where Interstate 65 intersects State Road 25 today, and followed the southern side of the Wabash River into Lafayette. The Wabash rail line ran southwestward out of Lafayette parallel to the current State Road 25, then passed through Attica and Williamsport on its way to central Illinois.[13]

Given the number of steam rails connecting Tippecanoe County to the rest of the state and country, it is accurate to say that daily commerce and the flow of goods into Lafayette was dependent on the daily service of these four steam railroads. Factories in Tippecanoe County required the rails for bringing raw materials into the county and transporting finished products out. In addition to the steam rails, there were two interurban electric car services that ferried people and, to a lesser degree, products into and out of the county. The Terre Haute, Indianapolis and Eastern (THIE) traction

An interurban railcar from the Terre Haute, Indianapolis and Eastern Traction Company, which ran from Indianapolis to Lafayette via Lebanon, Frankfort and Mulberry, entering Tippecanoe County at Dayton. This enclosed configuration of interurban cars was typical for many lines within Indiana in 1913. *Image courtesy of the Tippecanoe County Historical Association.*

This 1911 photograph shows the type of car that ran on the Fort Wayne and Northern Indiana Traction Company lines through Lafayette, West Lafayette and on the spur that provided service to Battleground. This photograph was taken on North Third Street in downtown Lafayette. *Image courtesy of the Tippecanoe County Historical Association.*

This photograph shows the Fort Wayne and Northern Indiana Traction Company track that ran along the Wabash River from West Lafayette north to Battleground along a sand and dirt road that is North River Road today. *Image courtesy of the Tippecanoe County Historical Association.*

company ("traction" referring to railcars driven by electricity supplied by a power plant) carried Tippecanoe County residents to and from Indianapolis via Frankfort, Lebanon and Zionsville multiple times a day. The Fort Wayne and Northern Indiana Traction Company ran an electric interurban rail line from Fort Wayne to Lafayette, following the path laid out by the former Erie Canal, and it connected Lafayette daily commuters to Logansport, Wabash and Peru. A third short electric line was constructed between West Lafayette and Battleground along North River Road, providing service between the west side's Main Street and the Wabash Valley Sanitarium, Tecumseh's Trail Park near the Indiana Soldiers' Home and Battleground.[14]

By 1913, the daily lives of most residents in Tippecanoe County, especially in Lafayette and West Lafayette, were dependent on the efficiently scheduled steam and electric rail systems. Any disruption to the rail system in 1913 would have been roughly comparable to the closure of interstate and major state highways today.

The Wabash River and Its River Communities

Lafayette and its surrounding communities were no strangers to Wabash flooding. In the earliest days of Tippecanoe County's settlements, maps show a small community located on the western Wabash Riverbank, directly across from Lafayette. On some old maps, the community is named "West La Fayette," and on others, it has no name. The few settlers of this community built their homes on a riverbank that was lower than it is today, and as would be expected with homes or structures built in what is now known as a "floodplain," the buildings were soon washed away by spring floods. The few buildings that were rebuilt on the low land were repeatedly washed away by subsequent spring floods for years until the mid-1800s, when the site was abandoned by any large-scale development, and the communities of Chauncey and Kingston took root on the higher ground of the west escarpment of the Wabash River Valley.

Significant damage-producing Wabash River floods in Lafayette prior to 1913 occurred on June 11, 1858; August 5, 1878; and March 15, 1907, although the record for high-water flooding was held by the flood of February 17, 1883. The 1913 flood exceeded the record-holding 1883 flood

West Lafayette, at the top of the Chauncey Hill, looking east. The road running along the left side of the building is South Street, and it marked the southern boundary of the four blocks that constituted the original Kingston community. State Street, to the right of the building, ran down Chauncey Hill and onto the Main Street Levee. The original community of Chauncey would have been down the hill and to the left of State Street. The rails and overhead electrical wires were for the streetcars of the Fort Wayne and Northern Indiana Traction Company. *Image courtesy of the Tippecanoe County Historical Association.*

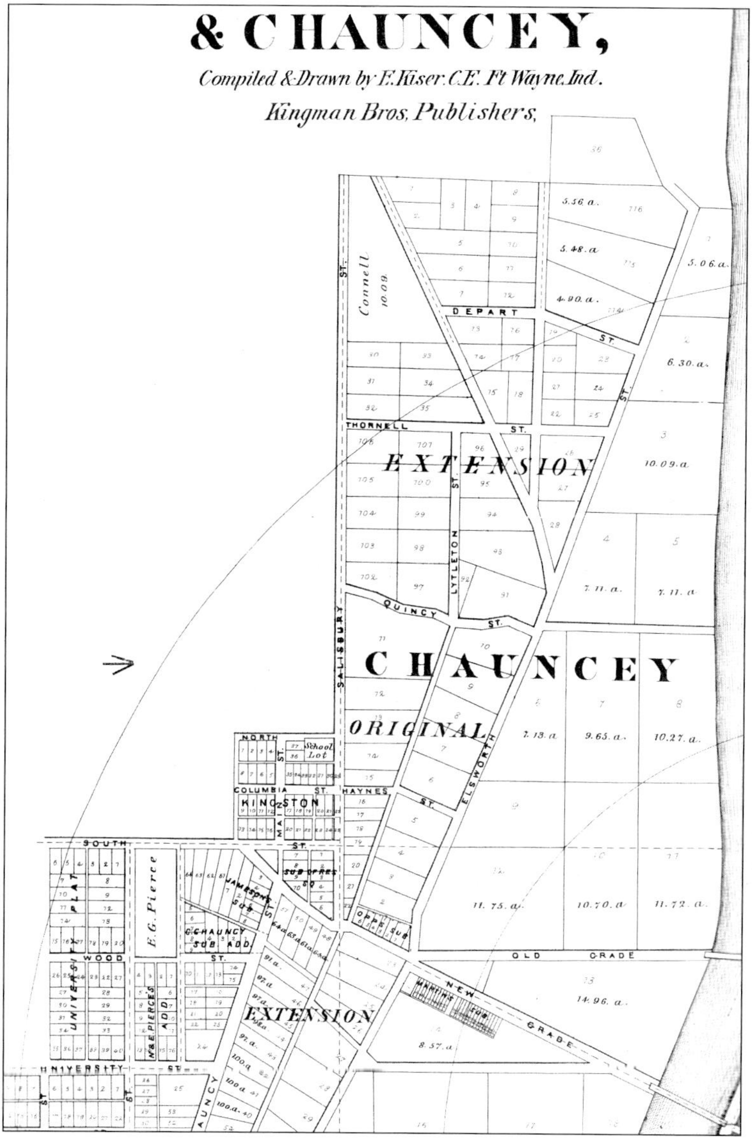

A scan of an 1878 map of the communities on the west side of the Wabash River (shown on right edge of the map). The Chauncey family laid out the original town of Chauncey in 1860; it was bordered to the south by State Street, to the north by Quincy Street, to the west by Salisbury Street and to the east by the river. By 1878, the original Chauncey, as well as its "extensions," occupied most of the land on the Wabash River from the railroad bridge to Thornell Street (now Stadium Avenue). The four square blocks of Kingston were platted in 1855, just west of Chauncey. Although Kingston is shown on this 1878 map as being separate from Chauncey, by 1870, it had been incorporated into the town of Chauncey. In 1888, Chauncey became West Lafayette. *Scan made by the authors.*

by twenty-two inches in Lafayette, and it exceeded all previous records at Peru and Logansport.[15] The record-breaking flood of 1883 resulted from an ice jam in the Wabash River downstream from Lafayette creating a blockage on the river and causing water to back up behind the jam, flooding the Lafayette community. In contrast, the 1913 flood was attributed to the heavy rainfall over the 7,300 square miles of Wabash River watershed in Indiana and Ohio from March 21 to March 26, 1913, resulting in a catastrophic volume of water being funneled into the Wabash and sent downstream.[16]

Maps and photographs of both sides of the Wabash River reveal a different topography in 1913 than what is observed today. In 1913, the east bank on the Lafayette side contained the steamboat wharfs that used to bustle with workers unloading and loading goods from boats and paddle wheelers. With the advent of reliable rail transportation, the steamboats moored along the wharf were replaced by houseboats, personal watercraft, boathouses and the occasional paddle wheeler moored to pilings, buildings, short piers and docks in various states of disrepair. Two lumberyards that were originally established next to the river for ease of shipping lumber products downstream when boat shipping was the economical way to ship lumber still stored their inventory within a few yards of the riverbank. Alongside the various wood-framed storehouses and livestock holding pens were more substantial brick warehouses and the power plant for the Fort Wayne and Northern Indiana Traction Company. Stables, business buildings, churches and residential structures were built just slightly farther inland beyond Second Street, but the gradual elevation between the river and the base of the eastern escarpment meant that these structures were not appreciably higher than the riverbank. As stated previously, by 1913, the former Wabash and Erie Canal in most of downtown Lafayette south of Cincinnati Street had been partially or completely filled in, and maps from around 1913 show that most of Lafayette's east–west streets, other than Main Street and Brown Street, crossed the former path of the canal on fill dirt covered by crude street materials, such as gravel.

The "bottomland" on the west side of the Wabash was not appreciably higher than the riverbank, so the two main roads from the west side leading to the Brown Street and Main Street Bridges, and the raised railroad bed embankment leading to the Big Four/New York Central Railroad Bridge, were all elevated above the surrounding west side bottomland. The elevated roadways were commonly referred to as the Main Street Levee and the Brown Street Levee. The west riverbank between the Brown Street Levee and the Main Street Levee was also slightly elevated, forming a protective

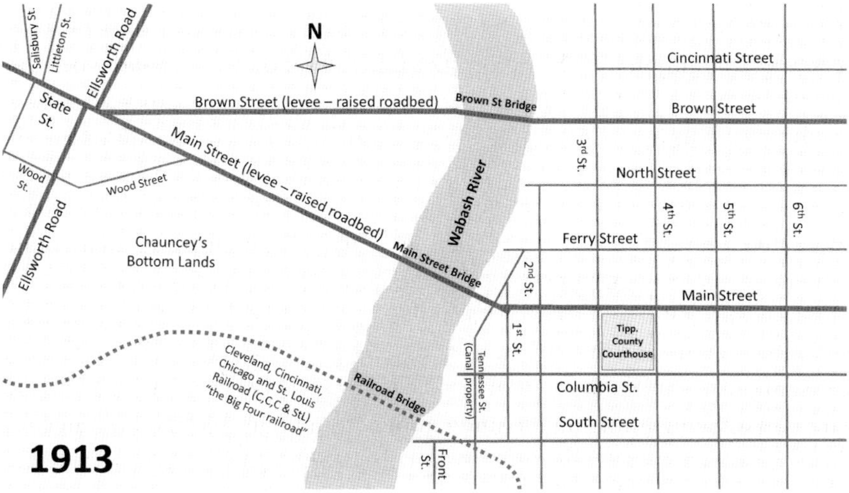

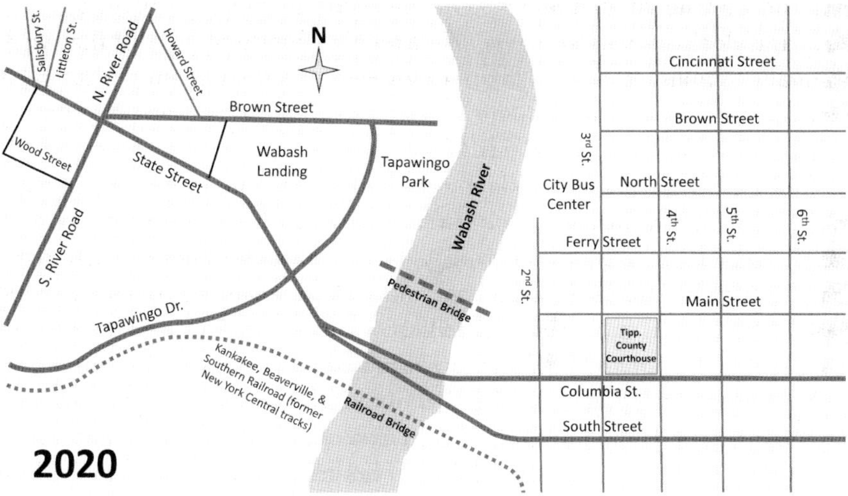

Top: This map shows the riverside communities of Lafayette and West Lafayette as they appeared in 1913. *Map constructed by authors.*

Bottom: This map shows the same area illustrated in the top image as it appears in 2020. *Map constructed by authors.*

triangle of elevated levees to protect the lower land between Main Street and Brown Street. The west bank, between the foot of the Main Street Bridge and the Big Four Railroad Bridge embankment, also formed a similar levee, effectively walling off the river from the Chauncey Bottomlands between the railroad embankment and the Main Street Levee. Although the banks along

A view from Lafayette toward West Lafayette. The elevated railroad embankment snakes off to the upper left. The Main Street Bridge is in the center right. Between the Main Street Bridge and the railroad embankment is the large barn and stable complex of the Lafayette Transfer Company, which was situated in the Chauncey Bottomlands. *From the postcard collection of Arnold L. Sweet.*

the west side had been elevated some above the river, the levee between Brown Street and Main Street was lower than the levee between Main Street and the railroad bridge, making it a weak point of defense against a rising river level. Thus, when flooding occurred, it tended to fill the land north of Main Street first, followed by the Chauncey lowland between Main Street and the railroad embankment.

The Brown Street and Main Street Levees afforded a sense of protection against high river levels, hence feed stores, grocers, automobile garages, a few homes and even a veterinary livery sprang up along the well-traveled Main Street and Brown Street Levees. Businesses also moved into the Chauncey Bottomlands south of Main Street, and multiple structures, including the large West Lafayette Coal Company coal barn, grew up in the basin between the Main Street and Brown Street Levees. Ellsworth Road, which is known as River Road today, formed the western rim of the lowlands and marked the foot of the western escarpment, which is often referred to today as Chauncey Hill or State Street Hill. Through either an engineering oversight or another reason, the lowest point of the Main Street and Brown Street Levees was near where the Main Street Levee met Ellsworth Road at the base of Chauncey Hill. This topography would play an important role in the damage and drama associated with the 1913 flood.

As March moved toward Easter weekend, which was promised by the U.S. Weather Service to be pleasant and sunny, life continued on in these river communities—much as it had the day before and the day before that. However, in the western part of the United States, a weather phenomenon was gathering that would change life dramatically for these communities in the following days.

Chapter 2

SPRING 1913

The Story Begins

It was the spring of 1913. Woodrow Wilson was succeeding William Howard Taft as the twenty-eighth president of the United States. Across the ocean in Europe and at home, the women's suffrage movement was blamed by the newspapers for causing havoc and destruction, including bombings, in their fight for the vote. The Sixteenth Amendment had just been passed, authorizing the federal government to impose and collect income taxes, and elsewhere in Washington, D.C., an obscure fifth cousin of the former president Theodore Roosevelt was appointed assistant secretary of the navy; his name was Franklin D. Roosevelt. Problems were brewing in Mexico with the return of Pancho Villa, and tensions were building throughout the world that would lead to the Great War—World War I. The local Lafayette newspapers carried retrospectives of the Civil War in their "50 Years Ago on This Day" segments. The impeachment of the governor of New York was splashed across the front page, and advertisements for all the latest ladies' fashions filled the center sections in anticipation of Easter Sunday. However, elsewhere in the country in the spring of 1913, and unwritten in any newspaper, nature's springtime forces were gathering for a weather event that would affect thousands of Americans.

As a general rule, the geographical area occupied by the continental United States experiences a wider range of weather phenomena than almost any other continent in the world. Unlike Europe, where high mountain ranges and other topography interfere or divert weather-producing air masses, the central part of the United States that constitutes the Great Plains and the Midwest is an open door that allows cold arctic air masses from the North Pole and warm, humid subtropical air from the Gulf of Mexico to collide and generate thunderstorms, tornadoes, blizzards, hail, tropical heat and bitterly dry cold.

The winter of 1912–13 was overall quite mild for the eastern United States. The climatological data report by the Lake Region of the Climatological Service (U.S. Department of Agriculture) characterized January 1913 as having "daily mean temperatures considerably above the normal," with the greatest deviations occurring in New York and Vermont, where the temperatures were between nine and thirteen degrees Fahrenheit above average.[17] February 1913 was described as "comparatively uneventful," with no exceptionally severe storms but temperatures and precipitation levels that were lower than normal. The cold temperatures experienced in February extended into the beginning of March 1913, in which record lows were recorded during the first seven days of the month. However, as the month progressed, the arctic cold air mass retreated in advance of much warmer and far more humid Gulf air masses, causing temperatures throughout the Ohio River Valley and plains states to reach into the seventies. This warm weather allowed the snowpack, which was relatively meager in many locations, to melt and the frozen ground to thaw, saturating the ground with water.

FRIDAY, MARCH 21, 1913

On March 13, 1913, the first of a series of storms, represented as low pressure systems, came in from the Pacific Northwest, tracked across the center of the plains and up the Ohio River Valley. These systems caused tornadoes from Louisiana to Georgia and produced gale-force winds throughout the Ohio Valley, the Midwest and the Great Lakes region. When the citizens of Tippecanoe County went to bed on the evening of Thursday, March 20, 1913, there was a light drizzle. They awoke a few hours later on Friday morning, around 5:00 a.m., to the sound of hurricane-force winds beating against their windows, uprooting trees and destroying wooden buildings and structures in what the *Lafayette Daily Courier* called "the worst gale that has visited Lafayette since the one that swept the Main street Levee in November 1911."[18]

Henry C. Walters, like most other Lafayette citizens, was roused from his bed by the wind hammering at his windows. He had been tending to his ill wife for several days and decided around 6:00 a.m., during the reported peak of the storm, to chance walking the short distance from his apartment over the Centennial Grocery in the 727 block of Main Street to Chambers Creamery to purchase some milk for breakfast. As he walked west on the north side of Main Street, no doubt with his head down and collar pulled tightly up against the cold wind and sleet, he likely heard a loud crack as he walked past Foster's Furniture and Carpet at 622 Main Street. The large wooden sign that extended across the front of the furniture store was ripped loose in the wind and hurled toward Henry, striking him hard on the left side of his head and pinning his unconscious body under the heavy board. In the dark of the spring morning, Henry Walter's body was found under the board by Chris Kalberer, who, with the help of others who braved the gale, lifted the board and hauled Henry into the Reitemeier Barbershop next door. The phone inside the building was inoperable, as the wind had taken down the phone lines, so Kalberer went out into the storm again and traveled the few blocks to the police headquarters to get help. The service wagon that served as an ambulance arrived shortly and took Henry to St. Elizabeth's Hospital, where he was attended by the well-known physician Dr. George Beasley. Unfortunately, the combination of the heavy bleeding caused by a large gash along the left side of Henry's head and the crushed-in parietal bone proved fatal, and he died shortly after arriving at the hospital, leaving behind his wife of thirty-two years and his three grown sons.[19]

Henry Walter's death was the only one related to this particularly ferocious spring storm in Tippecanoe County. However, property damage was extensive across Tippecanoe County. In addition to the gale-force winds, temperatures had plummeted over Thursday night, and by Friday morning, the temperatures were below freezing. The rain of Thursday evening had turned into sleet and snow, compounding the discomfort caused by the loss of electricity and heat and damage to roofs and buildings that exposed their interiors to the freezing elements.

The gale-force winds lifted many peaked roofs off their supporting walls, owing to the house-building techniques commonly used in the late nineteenth and early twentieth centuries. Many tin roofs of more modern construction did not fare any better, and there were several reports of the tin being "rolled up as neatly as if human hands had done the work."[20] Hundreds of brick chimneys, likely weakened with age, crumbled onto roofs and into the streets.

Out in the rural areas of Tippecanoe County, wind-driven pumps were ripped from the ground, fences were flattened and chicken coops and farm outbuildings could be seen rolling across farm fields ahead of the gale. Toppled trees and telephone poles lined the interurban rail lines of the Indianapolis and the Fort Wayne Traction Companies and halted all movement along the rail lines, further cutting off communication and the movement of people and goods between communities.

Stories filtered in about horses and their delivery wagons being blown over, wagon drivers turning back from crossing the Main Street Bridge for fear of being blown into the Wabash and narrow escapes from hurling debris. All the buildings on the west side along or between the Main Street and the Brown Street levees sustained roof or structural damage, including the Lafayette Sales Company livestock barn, the Lafayette Fence and Machine Plant, the Ash Pilling building and the Morgan and Torrenga garage.

On Purdue's campus, the large clock in the tower of Heavilon Hall stopped after large pieces of slate broke loose from the mechanical engineering building's roof and were hurled into the clock.[21] Interestingly, a set of senior Purdue students experienced the gale personally while making wind pressure measurements for their senior thesis papers. The shack in which they were huddled on Stuart Field, the football field located next to the armory and where Hovde Hall of Administration now stands, blew apart in the wind. The Purdue greenhouses, which housed medicinal plants and rare botanical specimens, had many panes of glass either broken or blown out. Fortunately, staff who had reported for work were able to protect most of the valuable plants. The agriculture experimental station on State Street recorded sustained winds of forty-five miles per hour before the wind-measuring instruments were wrecked by the gale.[22]

Most of the telephone and telegraph lines were rendered inoperable because the telegraph and telephone poles were broken off at their bases by the wind or uprooted by the combination of the soft, saturated ground and the force of the gales. The *Lafayette Morning Journal* reported that the eight hundred telephones of the Lafayette Telephone Company were rendered useless because of the downed lines. The other telephone company in town, the Central Union Company, suffered a similar number of outages. Most of the rural telephone lines were down, effectively cutting off any communication with the smaller communities in Tippecanoe County. According to the *Lafayette Daily Courier*, telephone wires near Purdue fell across wires carrying live electricity and "fire shot out from many telephones." The resulting sparks of the crossed lines produced "an electrical display that was startling."[23]

Purdue's Heavilon Hall (the mechanical engineering building). The tower contained four clock faces on each side of the tower that were each seven feet in diameter. The clock's chimes regulated Purdue student life. The hurricane-force winds of March 21, 1913, stripped slate tiles off of the building's roof and hurled them into the clock, stopping it at 6:05 a.m. *From the postcard collection of Arnold L. Sweet.*

Among the downed telephone lines were the wires leased by the Associated Press (AP) and the United Press (UP) to gather and furnish national and statewide news to the Lafayette daily papers. Thus, with the severing of the AP and UP lines, no news of the damage to Lafayette could go out to the rest of the nation, nor could national or state news come into the county by these news wires.[24]

An electrical pole on the Main Street Levee hangs suspended by its wires after the hurricane-force winds broke it off its base on the morning of Friday, March 21, 1913. *From the postcard collection of Arnold L. Sweet.*

Although most telephone wires were down and no long-distance lines were available, a few local lines were still intact, and the phone company operators were still attempting to connect calls because Lafayette had some intermittent communication with other phone stations within the state. However, during the height of the storm, half of the huge roof of the Lafayette Telephone Company at South and Fourth Streets was lifted off by the gale-force winds and placed, mostly intact, on the building adjacent to the phone company building. This left the third floor of the phone company building completely open while switchboard operators on the second floor continued to try to work the remaining phone lines. As the water from the storm began to flow through the third floor and into the switchboard floor, the manager and the operators covered the electronic switchboards with canvas and beat a hasty retreat. With that, almost all wire communication ended.[25]

In 1913, Tippecanoe County had a wireless radio station on South Fourteenth Street, near the county fairgrounds. With all telephone and telegraph wires down, the wireless became one of remaining modes by which Lafayette could communicate quickly with the outside world. Unfortunately, during the height of the gale, two tall iron-masted antennas composed of two-inch-diameter piping broke at the pipe joints, fell and damaged a nearby barn, thus ending any wireless communications in or out of the county.[26]

Deputy Sheriff C.W. Burroughs was awakened abruptly at 6:00 a.m., when the gale blew in the windows on the south side of his home and almost simultaneously blew out the windows on the north side. The gale swept everything in two rooms from one side of the house to the other, stripping pictures from the walls and piling up all of the furniture, a huge floor rug and the heating stove into a pile at the far end of the room. Deputy Burroughs's clothing was nowhere to be found, until he later discovered his coat, trousers and several shirts hanging from trees several hundred yards from the house.[27]

Ira Bennet was in his horse-driven wagon, making his rounds to carry mail for his Rural Route 3 patrons, when his horse suddenly collapsed at Twenty-Sixth and Main Streets. A telephone wire had blown off a pole and draped over the live electrical feed wire for the electric streetcar, immediately transmitting a fatal jolt of electricity to the horse. As the charged telephone line whipped about in the wind toward the wagon, Bennet jumped just in time to avoid the same fate as his horse.[28]

Out in Buck Creek in Washington Township, Peter Retterath was sheltering in his barn when the wind lifted the roof and shoved a wall of the barn on top of Peter, which was followed by the roof crashing on top of the felled wall. Peter was completely buried under the crushing weight of the rubble and only survived because the warmer weather of the previous few days had allowed the frozen ground to soften into a saturated layer of mud. It was "some time" before he could be rescued from under the fallen heavy timber, and while he sustained bruises and scratches, he amazingly suffered no broken bones or other serious injuries.[29]

At the Indiana Soldiers' Home north of West Lafayette on River Road, many trees were toppled, including the very old, large tree next to the adjutant's office that apparently housed many squirrels on the property. The *Lafayette Morning Journal* reported that "the little animals were greatly alarmed."[30]

By the end of the day on Friday, March 21, 1913, the wind had subsided, and it appeared that, once again, winter had firm control over the spring weather with its subfreezing temperatures. As people have always done after such weather disasters, they began to clean up, fix roofs, repair felled telephone and telegraph lines and put their lives back together. There were even jokes made that the weatherman's forecast for a cold Easter in spite of the warmer spring weather earlier in the week had actually come true. The residents of Tippecanoe County likely assumed that, despite the colder weather, Easter was coming on Sunday, and Easter always meant that warmer spring weather was not that far away.

SATURDAY, MARCH 22, AND SUNDAY, MARCH 23, 1913

The weather forecast for Indiana that was issued by the Washington, D.C. Weather Bureau and printed in the Saturday, March 22 *Lafayette Daily Courier* stated, "Fair and warmer to-night (Saturday); Sunday (Easter) unsettled and warmer; moderate variable winds."[31] The report out of Indianapolis promised, "Milady, in all her new spring toggery, will get to join in the great Easter parade tomorrow, for the weatherman has been generous and promised to deliver a fair and warmer day throughout Indiana."[32]

With the repair of some of the telephone, telegraph and leased news wires by late Friday, the newspapers were again able to gather and subsequently print information about the Friday gale that was circulating on the Associated Press and United Press news wires. Tippecanoe County citizens soon began to realize that the intense storm they had endured the previous Friday morning was not a weather phenomenon confined to their own community. The headline of the *Lafayette Morning Journal* that was delivered on Saturday, March 22, read, "One Hundred Reported Dead in Storm that Sweeps Nation." In addition to damage reports from Indiana and the surrounding states, the local newspapers had stories of death and destruction from Mississippi, Alabama, Texas, Louisiana, Arkansas, Kentucky and New York. Georgia reported two communities had been completely destroyed, with an estimated death toll topping seventy.[33]

They learned that the gales had done so much destructive damage to Chicago's telegraph and telephone lines that full service would likely not be returned until weeks of repair had been completed. In the meantime, telegraph communications were being routed through the few remaining lines by widely circuitous routes. In order for Chicago to communicate with Milwaukee, a distance of eighty-five miles between them, the messages had to be routed via remaining lines to Cleveland and then to Columbus, Ohio, down to Cincinnati, west to Kansas City, north to Omaha, then to Minneapolis and finally to east Milwaukee, a distance of over two thousand miles.[34] In Michigan, the highest wind speeds ever recorded were registered at eighty-six miles per hour in Detroit.[35]

The death toll in Indiana stood at two. In addition to Henry Walters, who was killed by the Foster's Furniture sign in Lafayette, Homer A. Vice, a Frankfort, Indiana cab driver in adjoining Clinton County, was crushed to death by a falling roof while he was on his way home from work.[36] Multiple reports filtered in of severe injuries in all parts of the state due to falling signs and bricks. Ironically for Henry Walters, the incidence of falling signs was extensive enough that one newspaper editor called for the statewide regulation of all heavy wooden signage to avoid repeating the litany of the injuries reported from people being struck by signs ripped loose by the gale.

As clean-up and repair began in the communities affected by the gales, a Canadian high-pressure system flowed into the upper plains, Midwest and Great Lakes region on Saturday, March 22, clearing the skies and keeping the temperatures near or below freezing. During the day, the high-pressure area and its accompanying blocking effect on any other low-pressure storms slipped quickly eastward, opening the door for a significant low-pressure storm in Colorado to move east.[37]

In contrast to the dry and cold weather of Saturday, March 22, Easter Sunday morning broke with southern winds ahead of the approaching Colorado low-pressure system, pulling warm air from the Gulf of Mexico. Temperatures in the Ohio Valley rose from thirty degrees Fahrenheit in the morning to over seventy degrees Fahrenheit by the afternoon.[38] Residents welcomed what seemed to be the beginning of the warmer spring weather.

Unbeknownst to most residents of Tippecanoe County, the warm, humid air mass also represented an atmosphere that was unstable and full of potentially destructive energy. Sustained southern winds of thirty-five miles per hour, with gusts above fifty miles per hour, were first reported in Kansas on Easter afternoon, resulting in huge dust storms. The storm intensified as it moved eastward, morphing into a line of severe storms capable of producing deadly tornadoes.[39]

Around 5:00 p.m. on Easter afternoon, the first of the tornadoes tore across the fields of Nebraska and into the town of Greenwood, which is located about forty miles southwest of Omaha. Survivors in Greenwood reported that the town was leveled by two tornadoes, one that came from the south and another that came from the west. The southern tornado continued northeast into downtown Omaha, while the western tornado proceeded east, where it destroyed several towns in Iowa.[40]

Prior to the arrival of the storm front, Omaha residents had enjoyed a warm Easter Sunday afternoon, with intermittent showers and occasional sunshine. Just prior to 5:45 p.m., dark clouds rolled in; the barometer dropped, indicating the approaching storm; and the temperature plummeted ahead of the storm line. Most of the citizens of Omaha were not aware of the rapidly moving storm front, and when the tornadoes hit, most had little time to find shelter in cellars or solid structures. The tornado cut a four-and-a-half-mile-long and one-quarter to one-half-mile-wide path of destruction

This photograph of the Omaha tornado was widely circulated on postcards. The tornado cut a quarter-mile-wide destructive path four and a half miles long through the middle of Omaha, Nebraska. The storms continued eastward and hit Terre Haute, Indiana, and Tippecanoe County. *Photograph from the collection of Pete Bill.*

diagonally across the city, levelling both the humble cottages of the western lowlands and the affluent mansions of Omaha's hilly northside.[41]

Stories abound of Omaha citizens being suddenly accosted by the tornado in the middle of their everyday lives. The tornado seemed to materialize out of nowhere in downtown Omaha as a "white balloon," and it caught a group aboard a streetcar near the Idlewild Club. The quick-thinking conductor ordered everyone onto the floor in the center of the car. Debris, heavy wooden planking and beams and even a carriage were thrown against the streetcar, shattering all of the windows but sparing the occupants, who not only survived but also emerged relatively unharmed.[42]

The adjacent Idlewild Club, a pool hall that was a gathering spot for the African American community in the near-north side of Omaha, was unfortunately the location of the greatest loss of life during the twister. Eight men were playing pool with a small crowd of onlookers when the low-frequency roar of the approaching tornado was heard. The men tried to take shelter in the basement, but the tornado lifted off the roof and plunged it back into the building, crushing the occupants. The woodstoves that were being used to heat the hall overturned and set the debris on fire, sealing the fate of those who were trapped inside. Thirteen bodies were reported as

The brick walls of the Plymouth Congregational Church at Boulevard and Spencer Streets in Omaha, Nebraska, were no match for the EF4 (Enhanced Fujita scale, level 4) winds between 166 to 200 miles per hour. *Photograph from the RPPC collection of Pete Bill.*

The tornadic wind was strong enough to lift C.F. Hopper's house at 4203 Farnum Street in Omaha off its foundation and roll it, mostly intact, into a neighboring home. *Photograph from the RPPC collection of Pete Bill.*

A crowd gathered as searchers looked for bodies in the charred remains of the Idlewild Pool Hall in downtown Omaha. The tornado lifted the top structure of the building and then plunged it into the basement, triggering a fire that killed the sixteen people who were trapped in the debris. The Idlewild was the site for the single largest death toll from this tornado. *Photograph from the RPPC collection of Pete Bill.*

being found in the hall, although the *Lincoln* (Nebraska) *Daily Star* reported three days later that sixteen bodies had eventually been found in the burned and charred debris of the building.[43]

In an interesting twist of fate, the tornado drew within five blocks of the home of Dorothy King but spared her house. Had it not, Dorothy would not have lived to remarry, move to Michigan and raise the future thirty-eighth president of the United States, Gerald R. Ford.[44]

Based on the degree of destruction documented in the photographs and reports of the day, meteorologists today have estimated the Omaha tornado would have rated a level 4 on the Enhanced Fujita scale (EF4), suggesting the wind speeds were between 166 and 200 miles per hour. The death toll in and around Omaha eventually numbered 103, with an additional 49 deaths reported elsewhere in Nebraska and Iowa.[45] In Omaha alone, over eight hundred homes were wrecked and another two thousand were damaged, resulting in an estimated $8.7 million worth of damage.[46]

Unlike today, when weather prediction is aided by almost instantaneous communication and views from weather satellites in orbit, in 1913, weather forecasting was based primarily on storm reports sent by telegraph from weather stations located to the west, the direction from which the storms typically approached. In the case of the Easter 1913 tornadoes that devastated Omaha, Nebraska, any possible warning that could have been communicated to the communities east of Omaha was prevented when the main telephone and telegraph lines in the city were destroyed and rail service was disrupted. Word of the Omaha storm and subsequent weather warnings were eventually sent out via a messenger, who took a train to the nearby military base at Fort Omaha, where a wireless radio sent information to Fort Riley, Kansas, which, in turn, sent the information out over its intact telegraph lines to the rest of the world.[47] The Associated Press disseminated information nationally to Associated Press–affiliated bureaus only after receiving information from messengers who were sent from the Omaha news bureaus to Lincoln, Nebraska, by train. Thus, warnings of the impending tornadic storm never reached communities east of Omaha, including the communities targeted by the storm in Indiana.

At 9:45 p.m. on Easter, March 23, 1913, a tornado spawned by the same storm that came westward from Greenwood, Nebraska, and Iowa, slammed into the southern end of Terre Haute, Indiana, destroying over three hundred homes, injuring over 250 people and killing 21.[48] This tornado was

This basement is the remaining part of this house in Terre Haute, Indiana. The Terre Haute tornado was an EF3, with winds reaching between 136 and 165 miles per hour. Because it struck at night, no funnel cloud was seen, and no warning had been received from Omaha because the telegraph wires were down. The storm claimed twenty-one lives in Terre Haute. *Photograph from the RPPC collection of Pete Bill.*

estimated to have been at least an EF3, packing winds between 136 and 165 miles per hour and capable of leveling homes to their foundations.[49]

The storm system that struck Nebraska and Terre Haute was part of the deadly collection of storms that produced nineteen tornadoes and killed at least 241 people in the forty-eight hours between March 21 and Easter Sunday, March 23. The Deep South states of Georgia, Mississippi and Alabama reported 49 deaths during the earlier tornado outbreak on March 21, and in addition to Nebraska and Indiana, deadly tornadoes from this same storm system claimed lives in Iowa and Missouri on March 23. Even in cities where tornadic activity was not reported, the strong hurricane-force winds in Chicago and Milwaukee and Traverse City, Michigan, blew roofs off of buildings, moved houses off their foundations and overturned homes like children's toys. No states east of the Mississippi River, from Louisiana to Minnesota, were spared from this destructive storm system.

But as the deadly weekend concluded, citizens in the Midwest did not realize that the coming week would bring another deadly natural disaster to their communities.

Chapter 3
THE RISING WATERS

Monday, March 24, 1913

Although the Monday, March 24 headline in the twelve-page *Lafayette Morning Journal* read, "Death and Heavy Property Loss in Wake of Tornado," the information on the front page about Omaha and Terre Haute was confined to only two of the seven columns and competed with stories about the new treasurer of the United States counting the money held in the treasury in Washington, D.C., and the fortieth anniversary celebration of Lafayette's Trinity Church. Citizens of Tippecanoe County likely assumed these most recent reports of severe weather from Omaha to Terre Haute were typical spring weather and, while unfortunate, represented "yesterday's news," meaning Lafayette and its vicinity had been spared from the tornadic winds of that particular storm.

The deluge of rain on Easter Sunday in Tippecanoe County had been unexpected because the *Lafayette Daily Courier*'s Saturday weather predictions described a "pleasant and sunny Easter day." No doubt because of some angry backlash at the grossly inaccurate weather prediction, the *Lafayette Daily Courier* felt it necessary to remind its readers that it—and all other newspaper publications—simply conveyed weather information received from the federal weather predictions office and that blame for the "brilliant" Easter forecast lay with the federal office and not the office of the *Daily Courier*. With perhaps a tongue-in-cheek explanation, the *Daily Courier* attributed the missed rain prediction squarely on the shoulders of the federal "weather chief" Willis L. Moore, suggesting that the poor prognostication resulted because Moore "was not made the secretary of agriculture in President Wilson's cabinet."[50] Easter's forecast failure notwithstanding, the weather forecasts for Monday promised to include more rain, and looking out the window anywhere in the greater Wabash Valley area, it appeared the weatherman was correct this time.

On Easter, March 23, 1913, the morning river gauge readings of Wabash River water levels from Logansport to Terre Haute were slightly below normal for the time of the year, and before the Easter Sunday rains began, the river levels were dropping.[51] As the Easter Day tornadic low-pressure system left the Midwest, moved across the Great Lakes and off to the northeast, the citizens of the Wabash and Ohio River Valleys would normally have expected a dry, high-pressure system to follow, bringing sunnier skies and cooler temperatures on Monday, March 24. Instead, in an unfortunate meteorological twist of fate, another low-pressure system from the Northwest followed closely in the track of the Easter storm and combined with a second low-pressure system from Texas that pulled tremendous amounts of additional moisture up from the Gulf of Mexico and into the Ohio Valley and Great Lakes region on Monday, March 24. A stationary weather front set up right along the Ohio River Valley, marking the boundary between a Canadian cold air mass and the moisture-laden gulf air mass, the combination of which produced ideal conditions for tremendous rainfall. Thus, the heavy rain that began with the Eastern Sunday storm on the evening of March 23 continued through Monday, March 24. Between Easter afternoon and 7:00 a.m. on March 24, approximately three inches of rain fell in the Wabash River basin that extended from Attica to Logansport.[52]

Wallace Garrison's Interrupted Trip

The continuing rain in the early morning of Monday, March 24, must have given Wallace Garrison some reasons to reconsider traveling along the water-saturated, muddy trails that passed for roads in rural Carroll County. It was still dark as he hitched his horse to his buggy and began the trip from the town of Burlington to his home on the other side of Wildcat Creek. Visibility was poor in the dim light and pouring rain, so it was likely that Wallace let his horse find its way along the muddy track.

The community of Burlington is located halfway between Lafayette and Kokomo. The Wildcat Creek, where it courses near Burlington, is normally a small, pleasant stream, but it was large enough to have water flowing in it all year round. However, the rain of March 23 and 24, combined with the water runoff from saturated fields, was rapidly filling all the streams, creeks and rivers of the Wabash River watershed, turning the placid Wildcat Creek into a dangerous torrent. As Wallace Garrison's horse plodded along in the muddy slop, neither the horse nor Wallace apparently noticed that the bridge over Wildcat Creek had washed out overnight. Perhaps it was the low visibility caused by the dark clouds and pouring rain or perhaps it was Wallace Garrison keeping his head down to keep as much of the rain as possible from running down his neck and not looking ahead, but whatever the cause, Wallace Garrison and his buggy drove into the torrent of Wildcat Creek. Hours later, when Wallace was reported missing, searchers found only the drowned horse, still hitched to the buggy, lodged in a pile of driftwood in twenty feet of water. Wallace Garrison was never found. The Flood of 1913 had claimed its first local victim.[53]

DUCK HUNTING TRIP TURNS DEADLY

Abraham Elva Meyers also likely thought Monday morning's rainy weather, with its heavy, low-hanging clouds, was not ideal for the duck hunting adventure he and his two friends, the Rothenberger brothers, Ray and Roscoe, had planned for the day. Spring might have been meteorologically around the corner, but on that day, it was chilly and wet. Still, Roscoe, aged twenty-six, and his younger brother, Ray, aged seventeen, had just completed building a low-sided johnboat and were eager to ply the flooded lowlands along Wildcat Creek near their homes in Mulberry in search of ducks to hunt.[54] In spite of warnings by friends, the three men dragged their boat to the south fork of Wildcat Creek, south of Mulberry, where they found the creek flooded well beyond its banks and covering farmland far from its normal banks. They were joined by another companion, Joel Hanger, who also counseled them against going into the water.[55] Their plan was to hunt ducks by floating downstream to Wyandotte, keeping to the slower-moving water of the flooded lowlands and avoiding the mainstream torrent. According to Elva Myers, at 9:00 a.m., the four men pushed their johnboat from the muddy farm field into the floodwater.[56]

It was not long after launching that Joel Hanger decided the turbulent water was too dangerous and demanded to be put ashore. The men rowed to the water's edge and put Joel ashore near what the paper described as the App Bridge. The App Bridge was a rudimentary bridge that spanned Wildcat Creek's south fork, and it was located next to the property and creekside gristmill that was owned by O.P. App and his family. With Joel Hanger ashore, Myers and the two Rothenberger brothers pushed off and floated downstream, out of Hanger's sight.[57]

The flooded creek was reported to be almost a mile wide near the Wyandotte Bridge, making it difficult to identify the fast-flowing creek current from the slower-moving flooded lowland areas.[58] Apparently, the men ventured closer to the more turbulent northward-flowing main stream of Wildcat Creek, and shortly before passing under the Wyandotte Bridge south of Dayton, the johnboat got hung up on a partially submerged tree or snag in the swollen creek. The johnboat was a low, flat boat meant to be handled on calm water for recreational fishing or hunting and was not constructed to handle the type of turbulence the three men found themselves in. Pushed by the strong current, the shallow boat quickly overturned on the snag, dumping all three men into the cold, rushing water.

Elva Myers fought the current long enough to reach a projecting limb of a submerged tree, where he pulled himself up into the branches. Looking

The two well-dressed men, one of whom is holding a dog, are navigating the flooded streets north of Lafayette in a johnboat. The johnboat was commonly used on calm waters because its low sides and flat bottom made it unstable and dangerous to use in turbulent current. Such a boat was used by Abraham Elva Meyers and the Rothenberger brothers on their ill-fated hunting trip on Wildcat Creek. *From the postcard collection of Arnold L. Sweet.*

around, Elva saw the younger brother, Ray, flailing in the water, as he had been separated from the boat. Likely laden with heavy clothing and hunting boots, Ray was quickly submerged underwater, and Elva never saw him resurface. The older brother, Roscoe, had managed to hang onto the overturned johnboat, and the last Elva saw of him, he was being carried rapidly downstream, where he passed from view around a bend in the creek.[59]

Myers, clinging to the branches of the tree in the icy torrent, began yelling for help. It was not until noon that James Russell, who lived near the Wyandotte Bridge, heard his cries. Russell notified Peter Rothenberger, a distant relative of the Rothenberger brothers, that someone was in need to help in the river. Rothenberger went to the river and found Myers still clinging to the tree. Rothenberger called some neighbors to help, but they saw that Myers was too far from dry land (described as being about "ten rods" or 165 feet away) to be thrown a rope, and no boat was immediately available to attempt a rescue. Telephone lines were down in many parts of the county from the previous week's storm, so a messenger was sent by car to Mulberry, four miles away, to procure a boat. It took some time for a boat to be found and transported back to the flooded bank of Wildcat Creek. By early afternoon, a crowd had gathered at the edge of the water to shout encouragement to Myers to hang on until help arrived.[60]

It was not until shortly before 3:00 p.m. that the boat arrived. Dana Hoch of Mulberry tied a rope around his waist for his own protection in case he too was pitched into Wildcat Creek, and having been secured, he pushed the boat into the water and rowed to where Myers still clung to the tree in a semiconscious state almost four hours after being thrown into the cold waters.[61]

Hoch helped Myers into the boat, but Myers could not talk and could barely move, most likely due to hypothermia from the prolonged exposure to the cold water and temperatures. He was transported to his home by automobile, where he eventually recovered from his ordeal. A search of each side of the Wildcat failed to find either of the Rothenberger boys and was called off at midnight.[62]

Rising Water Interrupts Normal Life on Monday

Heavy rain continued to fall throughout the day. The *Lafayette Daily Courier* quoted one of the experienced Wabash River men as saying they had never seen the river rise so quickly and that they were surprised by the huge

The view looking down the Brown Street Levee toward the river from the corner of Ellsworth Road, Main Street and Brown Street. This photograph was likely taken on Monday, March 24, 1913, early in the flood. *Image courtesy of the Tippecanoe County Historical Association.*

amount of debris flowing down the river and accumulating around the piers of the Main Street and Brown Street Bridges. Purdue University would record three and a half inches of rainfall in the period between 5:00 p.m. on Saturday, March 22, and 5:00 p.m. on Monday, March 24.[63] The *Lafayette Daily Courier* reported that the Wabash River was rising at a rate of over a foot an hour, breaking all previous records.[64]

Throughout Monday, the buildings, homes and businesses along both shores of the Wabash River battled the rising water. River water began backing up into the drainage sewers, and pumps were employed to attempt to save the equipment and inventory in the buildings near the river. The Tippecanoe County Detention Hospital for patients afflicted with smallpox or other communicable public health threats was a building on the west bank of the Wabash River on the lowland just south of the railroad embankment. Sometimes referred to in the community as the "pest house" (in reference to a pestilence or plague), the single-story building was built on elevated piers to keep it above normal spring flooding. However, even with its higher elevation, the *Lafayette Daily Courier* reported that, by Monday evening, the river water was lapping at the first floor.[65]

A close-up of the previous photograph. The dirt-and-gravel Brown Street Levee slopes upward to meet the Brown Street Bridge in the background. Floodwater was just starting to flow across this low spot on the levee when this photograph was taken; eventually it would cut a gash across the levee, filling the basin between the Main Street and Brown Street Levees. This was probably one of the last photographs taken of the intact Brown Street Levee and Bridge. *Image courtesy of the Tippecanoe County Historical Association.*

The rising water was beginning to cover the streetcar tracks near the Wabash River in Lafayette and the tracks of the Lafayette-Battleground interurban line that provided electric rail service between Battleground and Lafayette. Because the power for these streetcars came from overhead wires, the streetcars could continue to run over low-flooded rails using "high-water" cars and trailers, in which the passenger compartments were positioned higher over the wheel chassis. However, by 6:00 p.m. on Monday, March 24, even these special cars were not enough to keep the transportation line open between Battleground and Lafayette, severing the service many people depended on to commute between the two cities.[66]

The transportation of people and freight from Tippecanoe County to the rest of the state was also coming to a halt by late Monday, March 24. The interurban rail lines that ran between Lafayette and Fort Wayne, and between Lafayette and Indianapolis, were also disrupted by high water. By Monday afternoon, even some of the major rail lines, such as the Monon, the Big Four and Lake Erie and Western Lines were unable to get rail

The Detention Hospital, or "pest house," was a hospital for patients with communicable diseases like smallpox. It was physically separated from the rest of West Lafayette by the Big Four Railroad embankment (which can be seen on the right). Despite the hospital being elevated on stilts, the flood quickly surrounded it and covered the lower floor with eighteen inches of water by Tuesday, March 25, 1913. *From the postcard collection of Arnold L. Sweet.*

This "high-water" interurban electric railcar from the Fort Wayne and Northern Indiana Traction Company ran from Battleground to West Lafayette along the Wabash River's western bank. High water near the Wabash Sanitorium on River Road likely stopped all service not long after this photograph was taken. *From the postcard collection of Arnold L. Sweet.*

service to or from Lafayette due to high water covering large sections of rail lines and rail bridges either in the process of collapsing or being threatened with collapse by the force of the floodwaters of the Wabash River and its tributaries.[67]

Between the damage to telephone and telegraph lines from the previous gale and the flooding of roads, bridges and rail lines, the outlying communities along the Wabash River in Tippecanoe County were rapidly being cut off from the rest of the of the world.

Chapter 4

THE RAIN CONTINUES TO FALL, THE RIVER TO RISE AND LIVES ARE LOST

Tuesday, March 25, 1913

On the morning of Tuesday, March 25, 1913, the citizens of Tippecanoe County awoke to continued rain. The news in the *Lafayette Morning Journal* was still focused on the destructive tornado damage in Omaha, Nebraska, probably reflecting the delay the storms had caused in getting news out from the affected area. Only one column of the front page of the *Lafayette Morning Journal* had any information about the local Wabash flooding, and that was an article relating the story of Elva Myers and the Rothenberger brothers. By early Tuesday morning, the Wabash River level was well above its eleven-foot flood stage, but at the time the Tuesday edition of the *Lafayette Morning Journal* went to press, the river water levels were still well below the levels of the record-setting 1883 flood that had been caused by a downstream ice jam.

Although records of rainfall in Lafayette indicate that the rain tapered off late Monday and into Tuesday, providing a respite from precipitation for Tippecanoe County citizens, the rain continued to fall east of Tippecanoe County in the upstream Wabash River watershed around Fort Wayne, Wabash and Peru, Indiana, producing record-high river levels in those communities.[68] The massive amount of water that had been poured into the Wabash River Valley upstream was headed rapidly downstream, toward Lafayette. As a result, the Wabash River continued to rise in Lafayette as fast as four inches an hour throughout Tuesday, creating even greater alarm for businesses and homeowners along the river. By early Tuesday, the east riverbank on the Lafayette side between the Main Street and Brown Street elevations was being rapidly eroded away, putting huge riverside inventories of lumber belonging to the Lafayette Lumber Company and the Henry Taylor Lumber Company in danger of becoming part of the floating debris swirling downriver. Workers from both of the lumber companies worked frantically to corral floating lumber and move remaining stock to higher ground before it was washed away. Farther to the south, along the river near the Connorsville neighborhood, the large Lafayette Box Board and Paper Company, often colloquially called the "Strawboard Company" or "Boxboard Company," had to cease operations early Tuesday morning because its pumps were unable to keep the frigid floodwater at a low enough level to allow work to continue.

On the west side of the river, the higher elevation of the Main Street and Brown Street Levees and their corresponding bridges still allowed west siders to walk, mostly dry-footed, to and over the rapidly rising river. All morning long, Purdue students and citizens of Lafayette and West Lafayette crossed the bridges in order to get a better view of the rising torrent. By early Tuesday, the swollen Wabash River had already begun to breach the elevated bank on the west side of the river between the Main Street and the Brown Street Levees. It began filling the basin of the low-lying ground between the two levees all the way up to the intersection of Main Street, Brown Street and Ellsworth Road. By noon, the breach in the elevated bank had allowed the river to swirl violently into the submerged levee area, lifting the Pruitt family home from its foundation on the Brown Street Levee and carrying it into the river, where it was smashed against the Main Street Bridge piers and the support structures for the Big Four/New York Central Railroad Bridge. Fortunately, the Pruitt family had moved from the house a few hours before the river reached the house.[69] This scene of floating structures being dashed against the piers and bridges would be repeated countless times in the following two days.

It was common for commercial boats, houseboats and other personal craft to be moored to both sides of the Wabash River, between the Main Street and Brown Street Bridges. As the river rose quickly on Tuesday morning, the strong flood current pulled at the mooring lines, either uprooting the posts or trees to which the boats had been secured or snapping the ropes, sending the vessels downstream. The big forty-foot-long houseboat that was owned by Thomas Christopher and used to store canoes broke loose from its west bank moorings near the Main Street Bridge early on Tuesday. Once it was free of its moorings, the

The Main Street Levee in West Lafayette, looking toward the Main Street Bridge on Tuesday, March 25. The crowd in the background is waiting for the horse-drawn wagon service to transport them beyond the swift-moving floodwater crossing the levee at its lowest point near Ellsworth Road. Within forty-eight hours of this photograph being taken, most of this area was destroyed. *From the postcard collection of Arnold L. Sweet.*

This photograph shows turbulent water flowing through the breach in the Brown Street Levee. The levee's guardrails have been washed away, and debris is accumulating around the West Lafayette Coal Company's barn. The floodwater's turbulence, which is evident in the photograph, illustrates the danger of navigating a boat in this water. *From the postcard collection of Arnold L. Sweet.*

huge boat spun down the river, careening like a toy on the turbulent water. Unfortunately, Martin H. Oats, an employee of Christopher, was onboard the houseboat trying to pump water out of the boat when it was ripped away from its moorings. Within seconds of the boat slipping its moorings, Oats realized that he was out of reach of the west bank, cutting off his only means of retreat. Since he had seen other boats and buildings ripped away by the flood smashed to pieces against bridge piers, Oats must have feared a similar fate as he made his way to the bow of the boat. The Wabash River at this point of the flood was high enough that there was barely enough room between the underside of the New York Central System or Big Four Railroad Bridge and the swirling river for small boats or partially submerged, floating buildings to pass. Fortunately, the river level was still low enough to allow the houseboat's bow to pass under the first span of the railroad bridge. As it did so, Oats leapt off the boat's bow, grabbed a part of the iron bridge's span passing just over his head and, with some effort, hauled himself up onto the tracks, where he made his way safely back to the west side.[70]

Later that day, according to an article in the *Lafayette Morning Journal*, a similar scenario played out. "Slim" Miller was on a houseboat moored to an east bank anchorage at the Lafayette side of the Main Street Bridge. He was working from the roof of the houseboat, trying to save other neighboring boats from being swept away by the rising current, when, without warning, the anchorage gave way, and the houseboat began floating quickly downstream, toward the railroad bridge. Unlike Martin Oats, who had escaped from his wayward houseboat earlier in the day, Miller was unlikely to perform a similar escape act because the water of the Wabash River had risen sufficiently enough that boats could no longer slip underneath the railroad bridge. The *Morning Journal* reported that the crowds who lined the banks saw the houseboat break loose and realized, in horror, what was about to occur. They shouted a warning to Miller, who, according to the newspaper, just waved back. When the houseboat, driven by the fierce current, struck the railroad bridge, it was shoved under the water and crushed. As debris floated south beyond the bridge, the spectators must have assumed the worse had happened to Slim. Instead, someone spotted Miller hanging onto the flange of the low-lying bridge span, submerged in the river water up to his waist. Slowly, hand over hand, Miller worked his way toward shore, where he was pulled out by onlookers. The river current had stripped Miller of his boots, but other than that, he appeared to be in good shape, and within a few hours, he was reportedly seen back at work on the riverbank, attempting

This photograph, taken from Lafayette, shows the flood near peak level. The Main Street Bridge decking is barely above the water. The houseboats moored to trees on the far side of the river subsequently broke loose and were smashed against the railroad bridge to the left side of the photograph. The sternwheeler *Cayuga* in the foreground was moored to a building on the Lafayette side and survived the flood. *From the postcard collection of Arnold L. Sweet.*

to save other boats and launches from a similar fate.[71] The Wabash's rising torrent claimed many fine-quality boats and launches moored along the east bank of the river at the Main Street Wharf on Tuesday, tearing them loose and smashing them to splinters against the railroad span. It was estimated that $5,000 worth of launches were destroyed.[72]

By early Tuesday afternoon, the lowlands basin between the west side Brown Street Levee and Main Street Levee was filled with water, and much of the Brown Street Levee itself was submerged under the debris-laden water. The stone piers that supported the Main Street and Brown Street Bridges and the railroad bridges that connected Lafayette to West Lafayette were having to endure both the tremendous river current and impacts of large amounts of floating debris. Unfortunately, the velocity of the floodwater and the force it exerted on these bridges was made worse by the natural narrowing of the river between the landings of each bridge. The accelerated velocity of the flooded river at these constriction points caused extraordinary erosion of the river bottom, scouring the dirt that surrounded and supported the stone bridge piers.[73] The deteriorating effects on the foundation of these piers were not readily visible from the bridges above or from the banks, so people continued to walk and drive back and forth across the bridges.

"WATER CRUMBLES STEEL STRUCTURE"

After lunch, Lafayette workers Paul Wangerin, a cashier and bookkeeper at the Burt-Haywood Company; Arnold Herbert, a junior member of the firm Kimmel and Herbert; and William L. Oilar, the advertising manager of the *Lafayette Morning Journal*, gathered at the east end of the Brown Street Bridge to watch the muddy torrent and marvel at the amount of debris slamming into the bridge. Wangerin suggested walking across the bridge to get a better view, but Herbert and Oilar declined. A little before 2:00 p.m. on Tuesday, Wangerin started across the bridge and was followed by Charles Burkhouse, a carpenter and West Lafayette resident living on Pierce Street.[74] Although the newspapers of the time often cited Charles's name as Charles Burhouse, the city directory of 1911 lists only a Charles Burkhouse living at 1913 Pierce in West Lafayette.

Although the Brown Street Bridge was accessible from the Lafayette side of the river as of early Tuesday afternoon, the Brown Street Levee on the west side of the bridge was completely submerged, cutting off all access to the Brown Street Bridge from the west side. From the eastern foot of the bridge, Herbert and Oilar watched as Wangerin and Burkhouse began to cross the Brown Street Bridge and noted how the river was rapidly cutting into the eastern riverbank, causing large chunks of earth to collapse and fall into the rushing water. Shortly after 2:00 p.m., Herbert and Oilar felt the ground around their feet begin to quiver as if shaken by an earthquake. To their horror, they saw the western stone bridge pier on the far side of the Brown Street Bridge begin to crumble into the river. Without the pier to support it, the two metal spans on the west side of the Brown Street Bridge began to twist, collapsing into the river with a horrible metallic moan.[75]

At the sound of the disintegrating stone pier and the twisting metal, Wangerin and Burkhouse, who were most of the way across the bridge on the west side, ran for the nearer western embankment of the bridge. Behind them, the stone pier of the bridge and the western 130 feet of ironwork toppled into the current.[76] Wangerin and Burkhouse barely made it off the bridge and onto the remnants of the western dirt embankment that formed the approach of the Brown Street Levee to the western side of the Brown Street Bridge. The earlier breach of the western riverbank between the Brown Street and Main Street Levees had allowed the river to flow into the lowland, covering most of the Brown Street Levee with rapidly flowing water a couple of feet deep. Wangerin and Burkhouse

This photograph, taken from the Lafayette side of the river, shows the gap between the remaining spans of the Brown Street Bridge and the remnants of the elevated embankment of the west side Brown Street Levee, where Paul Wangerin and Charles Burkhouse were rescued after the bridge collapsed. *Photograph from the RPPC collection of Pete Bill.*

were trapped on a small island, surrounded by the whirling current of the Wabash River. The water was still rising, and the small piece of land they were on was rapidly shrinking.

Dozens of people were still walking across the Main Street Bridge when the Brown Street Bridge collapsed. Fearing a similar fate for the Main Street Bridge, the horrified onlookers on the Main Street Bridge ran for their lives. Soon after the initial panic and excitement of the Brown Street Bridge collapse had passed, onlookers standing along the Main Street Levee realized that two men were trapped on the only remnant of the Brown Street Levee above water.

Wangerin and Burkhouse made one attempt to wade along where they thought the Brown Street Levee should be under the water, with the hope of reaching the dry land that they could see in the distance near Ellsworth Road. They waded for only a short distance before finding themselves in waist-deep water, and fearing that they would be swept away, they turned back to the embankment to wait for rescue.[77]

West Lafayette, looking east from the Chauncey Hill. The Morgan and Torrenga Auto Company garage in the center of the photograph marks the separation of the Main Street Levee to the right and the Brown Street Levee to the left. The building with "Baltimore Clothing" painted on the roof is the West Lafayette Coal Company's barn, which was owned by Amos Mustard and sometimes referred to as the "Mustard coal barn." *Image courtesy of the Tippecanoe County Historical Association.*

This photograph was likely taken a day earlier than the image above and is looking north across the front of the Morgan and Torrenga Auto Company garage building to the right. The johnboat in this photograph is rowing over the submerged Brown Street Levee. *From the postcard collection of Arnold L. Sweet.*

The Rescue

Spectators who had been lining the Main Street Levee procured canoes from nearby businesses and were attempting to launch them from the levee. But the turbulent water flowing across Brown Street and into the basin between the levees quickly overturned the crafts, dumping would-be rescuers into the swirling water. Despite the warnings against any further attempts to launch craft by those gathered along the levee, two Purdue students, Leland P. Woolery and George B. Ely, found a canoe and prepared to push off from the Main Street Levee and into the flooded West Lafayette Coal Company barn and office yard not far from where Main Street and Brown Street Levees met. Woolery was a first-year student from Indianapolis who was pledging the Phi Delta Theta fraternity on campus, and George B. Ely was a junior at Purdue.[78] The two college lads had paddled no more than thirty feet across the coal yard when the turbulent water capsized the canoe "like an eggshell," tossing both men into the cold, churning water.[79]

A photograph of Leland Woolery from the Phi Delta Theta composite in the 1913 Purdue Debris yearbook. *Scanned by the authors from their copy of the 1913 yearbook.*

Leland Woolery had discarded his coat before climbing into the canoe, but he was still clothed in winter garments that threatened to drag him beneath the water's surface. Leland managed to make his way to a treetop but was unable to hold on due to the fierce turbulence of the flood current. He went under, and when he resurfaced, he appeared to be unconscious and was being carried toward the main body of the river.[80]

Shortly after George Ely hit the water, he was caught in a swirling current that drew him toward the roof of the West Lafayette Coal Company barn, which was still partially above the floodwater. As the current swept him near the barn, he swam the short distance toward the coal barn's office roof and was able to grab onto a partially submerged electric light wire that ran from the office roof of the coal barn to the levee. He pulled himself along the wire, hand over hand, the rest of the way until he

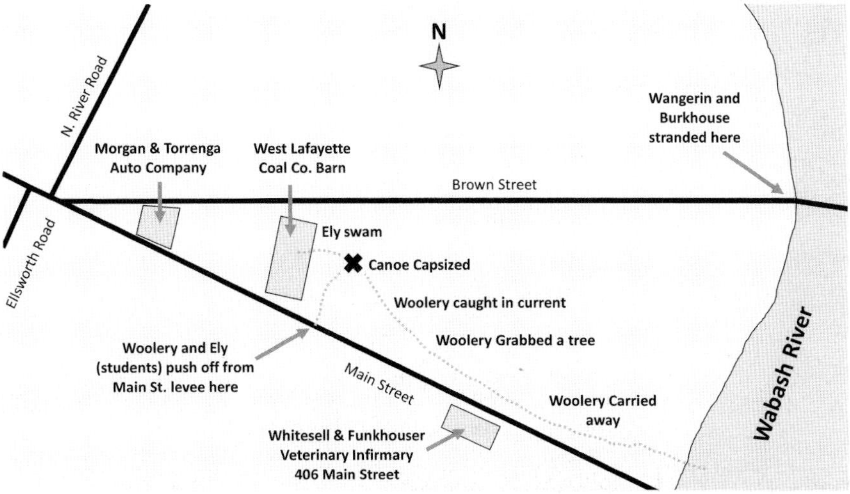

This map illustrates the path that was taken by George Ely and Leland Woolery in their failed attempt to rescue Wangerin and Burkhouse from the flooded embankment of the approach to the Brown Street Bridge. The "X" marks the point at which Ely and Woolery's canoe capsized and the two men went in different directions once they were tossed into the turbulent water. *Map created by the author.*

reached the barn roof and dragged himself out of the water. Although he was out of the water at the time, like Wangerin and Burkhouse, George Ely was trapped on an island that was barely above and completely surrounded by the raging water. From the turbulence Ely experienced, it was clear that if he tried to swim back to the Main Street Levee, the current would swiftly carry him away.[81]

By then a larger crowd, estimated by the *Lafayette Morning Journal* to number in the thousands—but more likely numbered in the hundreds—had gathered at the edge of the water at the base of the State Street Hill and Ellsworth Road. There was general concern that the coal barn roof George Ely was on would soon be swept away by the turbulent waters and that time was rapidly running out. Several attempts were made to throw a rope from the Main Street Levee to Ely (a distance of about one hundred yards). Each time, the rope fell short, and the current swept the rope away from the coal barn and back to the Main Street Levee. Then, a Purdue student climbed to the top of a utility pole on the edge of the levee to which the electric light wires from the coal barn office were still attached. The man cut one of the two wires from the pole and attached the end of a rope to the wire. Ely used the other end of the wire attached to the barn office to pull the rope to him.

The West Lafayette Coal Company coal shed and barn as seen from the Main Street Levee. After George Ely and Leland Woolery's canoe pushed off from near this point on the Main Street Levee and capsized, Ely managed to swim to the roof of the structure. The water, at that time, would have been three to four feet higher than it is in this photograph. *From the postcard collection of Arnold L. Sweet.*

From this point forward, accounts disagree on how the rescue of George Ely was actually achieved. However, the *Lafayette Morning Journal*'s account is far more detailed and more likely represents an accurate report because the newspaper had an employee present on the scene who participated in Ely's rescue. According to the *Lafayette Morning Journal*, after Ely disconnected the rope from the wire and secured his end of the rope to the coal barn roof, he crawled from the roof and into an opening of the barn's mow (barn attic for storage) that was next to the office, where he found another rope. Ely wrapped the second rope around himself and then secured the other loose end to the barn roof to act as an anchor should he be swept away during the rescue attempt. Captain Kluth of the Lafayette Police Department warned Ely not to attempt to try to pull himself to the Main Street Levee along the first rope, presumably for fear that the turbulent current would be stronger than his grip on the rope. Instead, another rope was handed to the Purdue student still stationed on the pole, and it was attached to the second electrical wire that led over to the barn office roof. Like the first rope, Ely pulled this second rope from the levee to him and attached the second rope to his body so rescuers on shore could use it to pull him toward dry land while Ely attempted to move along the first rope, hand over hand, toward the levee.

With a rope attached to the barn to serve as a safety anchor, a second rope connecting Ely to his rescuers on the levee and a third rope secured between the levee and the barn by which Ely would guide himself back to the levee, Ely let himself off the roof and into the turbulent current. The force of the swirling water caused Ely to quickly lose his grip on the suspended rope. As he disappeared under the water, rescuers on the levee frantically pulled on the rope attached to Ely's body and dragged him, mostly submerged, through the water, to within ten feet of the levee. There, Ely struck a tree and became temporarily stuck. However, Captain Kluth, Walter Clark from the *Lafayette Morning Journal* and two Purdue students waded over to the tree, cut the ropes that tangled Ely to the tree and pulled him ashore.[82]

According to the account detailed in the rival newspaper, the *Lafayette Daily Courier*, Ely employed a more innovative and exciting rescue method than

The Main Street Levee in West Lafayette, looking toward the Wabash River. The group of people in the middle of this photograph are attempting to rescue George Ely from the roof of the West Lafayette Coal Company's barn. The johnboat that was used to try to rescue Ely can be seen among the group. A student is up on the electrical pole to the left of the group. *From the postcard collection of Arnold L. Sweet.*

A close-up of the student perched on the crossarm of the electrical pole. The student had to cut the wire that ran from the pole to the coal barn, and he connected a rope to the wire so Ely could pull the disconnected wire and the rope from the levee to himself. *From the postcard collection of Arnold L. Sweet.*

the one described by the *Morning Journal*. Supposedly, after Ely had reeled in the first cut telephone wire with the rope attached, rescuers standing on the Main Street Levee attached a small boat to their end of rope, and Ely attempted to pull the boat to him. However, the current proved to be far too strong and turbulent, and Ely was unable to pull the boat to him. The boat was retrieved by the rescuers and disconnected, and a pulley was attached to the rope, which Ely subsequently pulled to him. According to the *Daily Courier*, after retrieving the pulley, Ely threaded the pulley over the rope and then the wire; then, he apparently tossed the rope back in the direction of the rescuers, who somehow retrieved it once again. The rescuers pulled the rope until the attached wire (still connected on Ely's end to the barn) was retrieved, and they reattached the wire to the utility pole, creating an intact wire between the barn and the levee with a pulley suspended from it. Supposedly, Ely then hung on to the pulley and rode it across the water to the levee like a modern-day zipline.[83] This more "thrilling" account of Ely's rescue is the one that was picked up and reported by most of the national newspapers as well as a majority of the books that were written about the event in 1913. While this version is more "newsworthy," there are some inconsistencies in the story that call the exciting version of the event into question. Regardless of how the rescue was actually accomplished, the fact remains that George Ely was successfully rescued from the barn roof.

The automobile that carried an exhausted George Ely immediately after his rescue from the Lafayette Company coal barn. Ely collapsed after being told that Leland Woolery had most likely perished. The automobile took Ely to his home at 459 North Grant Street in West Lafayette. *From the postcard collection of Arnold L. Sweet.*

When he was finally pulled to shore, Ely asked about Woolery and was told that he had been swept away to his death. Ely collapsed. He was loaded into an automobile and taken to his home at 459 North Grant Street in West Lafayette.

Meanwhile, Wangerin and Burkhouse were still waist-deep in water, awaiting rescue. Dr. Roy B. Whitesell was a veterinary surgeon who, along with fellow veterinarian Dr. Funkhouser, owned a veterinary facility at 406 Main Street, near the river. Seeing Wangerin and Burkhouse's plight, Dr. Whitesell procured a boat and, in what was described by the *Lafayette Morning Journal* as "the most daring feat ever performed by a boatman," set off from the partially submerged Main Street Levee near his livery. Although it was still turbulent, the water was not swirling as violently in the area closer to the river as it had been near the Coal Company barn, where Ely and Woolery had set out. Still, the current was very strong, and Whitesell rowed north across the flooded area between the levees against the current. He then crossed over the flooded Brown Street Levee and positioned himself so that he could then turn and move back with the current, toward the stranded men. Dr. Whitesell managed to successfully pilot the boat to a telephone pole on the Brown Street Levee, where he held the craft until Wangerin and Burkhouse were able to wade the few

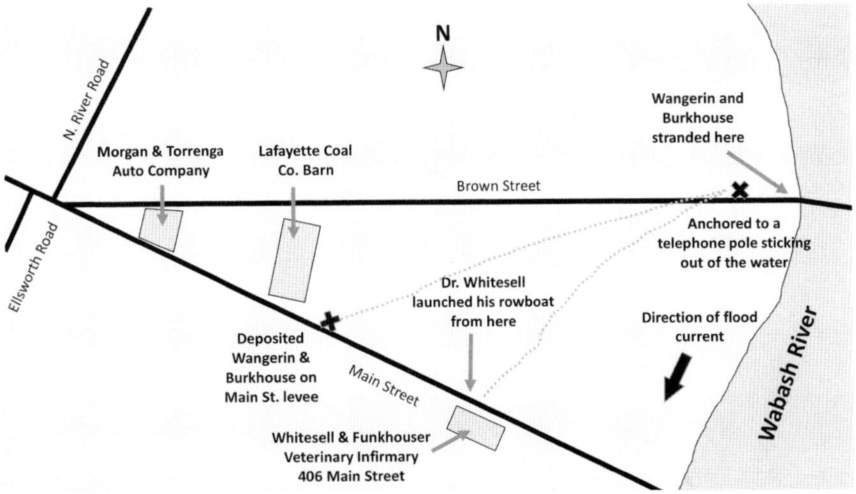

Dr. Whitesell launched a boat from his veterinary infirmary on the Main Street Levee and paddled against the flood current to reach Wangerin and Burkhouse on the west Brown Street Bridge embankment. Whitesell managed to anchor the boat to a telephone pole near Wangerin and Burkhouse. The two men waded the short distance to the boat, got in and Whitesell successfully navigated back to the Main Street Levee. *Image created by the author.*

yards to it and climb in. Dr. Whitesell then managed to successfully row back with the current to the Main Street Levee, where several men waded through the waist-deep water to pull the boat to shore and assist the men to the relative safety of the Main Street Levee.[84]

Loss of Bridges Isolates Tippecanoe County Communities

With the collapse of the Brown Street Bridge, all streetcar and vehicular traffic across the Main Street Bridge was stopped for fear of a similar collapse. It was not long after this (around 3:45 p.m. on Tuesday) that Lafayette mayor George R. Durgan took "personal charge" of the flood situation and ordered all traffic between Lafayette and West Lafayette to cease, including any foot traffic across the Main Street Bridge. The police force was called out to keep people from trying to cross the bridge, and eventually, a rope barrier was erected across the bridge's Lafayette side entrance, and guards were posted under the supervision of Superintendent Schafer. To keep the crowds back from the bridge approach on the Lafayette side, the barrier was moved and erected across Main Street at Second Street. With the Brown Street Bridge gone and the Main Street

Bridge blocked, a few souls attempted to cross the river on the railroad bridge, but Sheriff Fisher and his deputies were said to have "quickly put a stop" to that option.

By 4:00 p.m. on Tuesday, the second westernmost pier of the Main Street Bridge was beginning to settle, making the two steel spans resting on this pier tilt toward the rushing water below and twisting the bridge's steel truss structure. Wallace Marshall, the president of the Lafayette engineering company that had designed the bridge, stated that the greatest danger to the Main Street Bridge was the accumulation of driftwood against the bridge's pier, as it increased the surface area the pier presented to the flood current and increased the force of the flood against the piers.[85] However, in spite of the bridge's appearance, Marshall predicted that both the railroad and Main Street Bridges would likely survive.

By Tuesday afternoon, the river water that was flooding into the lowlands between the Brown Street and Main Street Levees was flowing rapidly over the Main Street Levee near Ellsworth Road, filling the lowlands, or Chauncey Bottomlands, south of Main Street. Unfortunately, like the abutments at the ends of the Main Street Bridge, the Big Four Railroad Bridge and its embankment had created a significant bottleneck through which the rising

Lafayette authorities positioned themselves on the east end of the Main Street Bridge to prevent further crossings for fear that the bridge would collapse at any moment. *From the postcard collection of Arnold L. Sweet.*

flood volume had to be funneled. The force of all this water slamming into the railroad bridge and embankment generated significant concern that the floodwater would soon uproot the railroad bridge and its piers, sending them downstream with the rest of the debris.

In addition to the direct assault of the river current and debris on the railroad bridge and embankment, the dirt railroad embankment was being eroded by the swirling current caused by the channel of floodwater pouring across the Brown Street and Main Street Levees. The floodwater was pouring into the Chauncey Bottomlands between Main Street and the railroad embankment and then flowing back into the main river channel along the north face of the railroad embankment.[86] The late edition of the Tuesday afternoon *Daily Courier* reported that river water was "seeping" through the dirt railroad embankment, prompting predictions that the entire railroad embankment would be swept away, severing a main rail line into and out of Lafayette.[87] By Tuesday afternoon, two hundred feet of the north side of the embankment base had already been eroded away.[88]

By Tuesday afternoon, it wasn't just the stopped traffic of the Big Four and Lake Erie and Western Lines across the New York Central System Railroad Bridge that was disrupting the movement of goods and people in and out of Tippecanoe County. Almost all steam railroad lines and traction lines like the interurban had stopped operations into and out of Lafayette. The only steam railroad line that was still operating out of Lafayette on Tuesday afternoon was the westbound leg of the Wabash Railroad, which used the stretch of track that ran west from Lafayette on higher ground that was farther away from the river along what is now State Road 25. It was the only major track that didn't have to cross any significantly flooded rivers or creeks as it headed west (with the exception of the Wabash River crossing at Attica whose bridge was still intact).[89]

Farther north of West Lafayette, along North River Road, the floodwater had completely covered the Lafayette Street Railway Battleground Traction Line near the Wabash Valley Hospital, or Sanitarium. By Monday, the rising water had already flooded North River Road at this location, and the water was rising up the hill, toward the relatively modern hospital. The hospital had been built on high ground near the Wabash River by the Seventh-day Adventists in 1906 with the idea that the tranquil location would complement the hospital's treatments, which focused on beneficial hydrotherapy and dietary treatments. While the hospital occupied the high spot of the twenty-five acres that comprised the hospital grounds, the attractive little station house that had been built by the traction line company was on lower ground

This photograph shows a Lafayette-bound Monon passenger train that was stopped because high floodwater was flowing over the tracks north of Lafayette. The passengers can be seen disembarking while waiting for the train to receive permission to back up to Battleground. *Image courtesy of the Tippecanoe County Historical Association.*

near the river, and by Tuesday afternoon, the river was threatening to lift the little house off its foundation and float it away. Sanitarium workers tried valiantly to secure the wooden building to its foundation, but the structure began to float up with the rising water. Even when the entire building began to float away into the main Wabash current, two workers from the sanitarium rowed out, put a rope around the little building and attempted to tow it back to higher ground. As would be expected with the force of the flood, this battle was quickly lost, and the handsome building floated to its doom. The *Lafayette Morning Journal* reported that except for the side of the sanitarium hospital that faced the western escarpment, the building was almost completely surrounded by floodwater. By the time the Wednesday morning *Lafayette Morning Journal* went to press, the water at the sanitarium was reportedly within fifty feet of main building, and by Wednesday afternoon, the *Lafayette Daily Courier* reported that the floodwaters were lapping at the front door of the hospital.[90]

Farther east of Lafayette, the swollen Wildcat Creek that had claimed the lives of the Rothenberger brothers on Monday was eroding away the bank that supported the western end of the Fort Wayne and Northern Indiana Traction Company Bridge near where Indiana 25 and Interstate 65 are today. This interurban line was a crucial passenger connection between

Workers near the Wabash Valley Sanitarium north of West Lafayette work on the rails of the Fort Wayne and Northern Indiana Traction Company interurban line that ran along River Road to Battleground. Within forty-eight hours of this photograph being taken, this area was under three to four feet of floodwater. *Image courtesy of the Tippecanoe County Historical Association.*

The interurban station depot at the Wabash Valley Sanitarium. The proximity of the interurban rails and the depot to the Wabash River made them both victims of the rising flood. *Photograph from the postcard collection of Arnold L. Sweet.*

Lafayette, Delphi, Logansport, Wabash, Peru and Fort Wayne. Unlike the Brown Street, Main Street or Big Four Railroad Bridges, which had been built with long spans supported by single-column stone piers, the traction line bridge was a trestle bridge, meaning it was composed of short segments of tract supported by multiple "bents" or triangular wooden pole frames that carried the span across the river or creek. The weakness of the individual bents as compared to the stone piers was compensated by having many more bents under the span to distribute the weight above.

Unfortunately, Wildcat Creek's torrent over the course of Monday and Tuesday tore out one bent at a time until, by Tuesday afternoon, fourteen bents had been uprooted and sent down Wildcat Creek to the Wabash River with the rest of the floating debris. Without the support, the trestle bridge's rails twisted and collapsed into the creek. With the traction line bridge destroyed and no one willing to venture across the nearby wagon bridge for fear of being washed away if the bridge collapsed, the transportation of people to and from locations east of Lafayette was effectively cut off.[91]

Even if bridges in Tippecanoe County were still standing, the approaches to them were underwater. The *Lafayette Morning Journal* reported that the bridge at Davis Ferry (now North Ninth Street in Lafayette) and the Jewettsport Bridge near Battleground (now the single-lane State Road 225 bridge across the Wabash River) were both standing but unable to be reached from either side.[92] A similar situation existed at the Granville Bridge south of Lafayette, which was described as "still on its piers," but the approaches had been cut away by the current of the Wabash flood.[93]

By midafternoon on Tuesday, the Lake Erie and Western Railroad superintendent, C.C. Arnold, determined that it would still be possible for one last locomotive and a single passenger car to travel safely across the New York Central System Railroad Bridge to help west side folks get back to West Lafayette before the rail bridge was shut down completely. Captain John Kluth and members of the police force went about downtown Lafayette, announcing that a special train would take marooned west siders across the bridge at 5:00 p.m. that evening. A large crowd had gathered on the east side by 5:00 p.m.—far more than could be accommodated by the lone railcar. It was felt that no additional cars could be safely added to the train, so a little after 5:00 p.m., a single heavily loaded passenger car was pulled slowly across the bridge. Passengers were reported as acting fearful as they crossed the bridge because they could see the Wabash River current seething just below the tracks. The train went as far as Grant Street on the west side, unloaded its passengers and reversed across the bridge to pick

A trestle bridge. Each wooden trestle pier was made of individual wooden pole "bents" that were connected laterally to support the horizontal bridge spans. Although trestle bridges were less expensive to build than bridges with stone or concrete piers, they were more susceptible to damage from floods or ice floes. *From the postcard collection of Arnold L. Sweet.*

The Fort Wayne and Northern Indiana Traction Company trestle bridge over Wildcat Creek progressively collapsed into the creek as each individual wooden bent was swept downstream. The steel-trussed wagon bridge with its sturdier stone piers can be seen intact in the background. *From the postcard collection of Arnold L. Sweet.*

This view of the Fort Wayne and Northern Indiana Traction Company trestle bridge over Wildcat Creek shows how the force of the floodwater sheared off the part of the bridge that was supported by wooden trestles, dragging the remains of the trestles and their rails downstream and leaving only that part of the bridge supported by concrete piers. *Image courtesy of the Tippecanoe County Historical Association.*

up a second load. This was repeated a total of three times, with the last car leaving Lafayette at 5:30 p.m. After that, all passenger rail service across the bridge was stopped.

With the shutdown of the railroad bridge early Tuesday evening, all means of travel across the Wabash River and its major tributaries, like Wildcat Creek in Tippecanoe County, had been disrupted, cutting off many communities from each other, including Lafayette and West Lafayette. As the *Lafayette Morning Journal* stated on Wednesday morning, "The only means of communication [with other communities outside of Lafayette] is by airship."

WEST SIDE MERCHANTS FLEE ADVANCING FLOOD

Merchants along the elevated Main Street and Brown Street Levees, as well as those businesses farther away from the Wabash but still in the lowland between the levees, had begun moving their equipment and merchandise to higher ground starting on Monday, and they continued throughout Tuesday morning. One of the larger employers of people on the west side was the Esterline Company, located in the Chauncey Bottomland to the south of the Main Street Levee. Founded in 1906 by John W. Esterline, a Purdue electrical engineering graduate and former department head of electrical engineering at Purdue, the company originally made magnets and recording devices. In 1912, Esterline was successful in developing a six-volt starting system for automobiles, and they were being manufactured on a large scale in the spring of 1913. Using a battery developed by the Willard Storage Battery Company in Indianapolis, Esterline's six-volt starting system was less complicated to use and had lower voltage than the thirty-two-volt system that had been previously developed for starting Cadillacs. Up to this point in automobile manufacturing history, most automobiles were started using a hand-crank system. Esterline's system was a great success when it debuted at the 1912 auto shows, and by late 1912, Esterline had built a large cinder-block factory building in West Lafayette, between the Main Street Levee and the railroad embankment, and employed between two and three hundred employees to meet the demand for Esterline's system.[94]

But by the early morning of Tuesday, March 25, 1913, the Wabash River had already flooded the land north of Brown Street, and the floodwater was flowing across Brown Street and into the land between the Main Street and Brown Street Levees, filling that basin. In addition, by Tuesday morning, the river had breached the embankment between Main and Brown Streets, allowing river water an additional route for the floodwater to pour into the basin. It wasn't too long before the filled basin between the Brown Street and Main Street Levees began to overflow the Main Street Levee, cascading down the other side of the levee and into the Chauncey Bottomlands near the intersection of Main, Brown and Ellsworth Streets. By mid-morning on Tuesday, the Esterline Company and other businesses in the Chauncey Bottomlands between Main Street and the railroad embankment had begun to see the water rising inside their buildings. True to their engineering roots, the engineers at Esterline were reported by the *Lafayette Daily Courier* to have been plotting a mathematical curve to predict how rapidly the incoming floodwater would rise inside the building. Of course, the engineers placed a caveat on their predictions, stating that if the raised riverbank levee between Main Street and the railroad embankment gave way, the Chauncey Bottomland would flood much quicker. The *Daily Courier* reported that the Esterline plant contained over $200,000 worth of electronic inventory, valuable machinery and finished product that was ready to ship. Anticipating the need to evacuate the building, the company had already moved and shipped over $50,000 worth of inventory for fear that it could be irreparably damaged by floodwater. By mid-afternoon on Tuesday, the shallow flow of

The Esterline Company was located in the Chauncey Bottomlands between the Main Street Levee and the railroad embankment. The floodwater rose to the bottom of the sign on the front of the building. Rather than rebuild his electronic parts factory after the flood, John Esterline moved the operations to Indianapolis. The company still exists in Bellevue, Washington, where it manufactures electronics for the aviation and defense industries. *Image courtesy of the Tippecanoe County Historical Association.*

floodwater that had been crossing the Main Street Levee and falling into the Chauncey Bottomlands had turned into a torrent, flowing like a waterfall into the lower ground. At 5:15 p.m. on Tuesday, the west riverbank levee between the railroad embankment and the Main Street Levee gave way, and the flooded Wabash River rushed through the gap, adding to the water that was already pouring over the Main Street Levee. The last man out of the Esterline building had to wade through rising floodwater that came up to his knees. By Tuesday evening, the Esterline factory and its sophisticated equipment and electronic stock were inundated, and the water was rising steadily toward the building's roof.[95]

Fifteen minutes after the riverbank levee stretching between the Main Street Levee and the railroad embankment gave way, the surging water tore the large sales barn in the lowlands from its foundation, and it floated, intact, toward the gap in the levee and into the raging Wabash River. Spectators watched as the large wooden building barreled down the river the short distance to the Big Four/New York Central System Railroad Bridge. Although some watercraft and submerged debris had been able to pass under the railroad bridge earlier on Tuesday, by late afternoon or early evening, the river level was almost up to the bottom of the railroad bridge, with little room for anything to pass under it. The uprooted barn floated on top of the water and entered the main channel of the Wabash River, where it picked up speed. With a tremendous crash, it slammed into the railroad bridge, taking out several poles and electric lines strung across it. The splintered structure was forced under the bridge and emerged on the other side, where it flowed into a natural eddy in the water surrounding the detention hospital. For the duration of the flood, debris that passed under the railroad bridge continued to accumulate at this site on the west bank. Because of the eddy and the natural accumulation of floating debris, the river area in front of the detention hospital became a site where searchers looked for the bodies of those who had been claimed by the flood.

Water Everywhere, But Drinkable Water Is in Short Supply

By Tuesday morning, businesses on the Lafayette side of the river were still running their pumps at full speed in an attempt to save their inventory, buildings and equipment from the advancing edge of floodwater that was creeping up the streets of the riverside business district. By 2:30 p.m. on Tuesday, March 25, John E. Camardy, the superintendent of Lafayette's modern waterworks and pumping facility located on Canal Street near the river north of Brown Street, announced that the rising flood would soon extinguish the boilers, rendering the steam-driven water pumps that took water in from the Wabash River and delivered it to the city inoperable. The water drawn from the wells located on the Canal Street Pumping Station waterworks grounds was stored temporarily in a 182,000-gallon covered holding cistern adjacent to the pumping station. Pumps powered by the steam generated from coal-fired boilers moved the water from the holding cistern to the 4,200,000-gallon concrete-sided Columbian Park Reservoir located 208 feet higher up the eastern escarpment and a little more than mile from the pumping station. Normally, during the day, most of the city's water and water pressure was supplied directly from the water stored in the Columbian Park Reservoir. The Lafayette residences on top of the eastern

The riverside Lafayette Waterworks in the early stages of the 1913 flood. The small circular building to the right of the main building is the cistern that held the water that was drawn from the wells. Steam-driven pumps moved the water from the cistern up to the Columbian Park Reservoir. When the flood extinguished the waterworks' boiler fires, the Columbian Park Reservoir could no longer be refilled. *From the postcard collection of Arnold L. Sweet.*

escarpment did not have the benefit of gravity to provide the water pressure needed to run water from their taps and relied instead on an auxiliary pump at the Columbian Park Reservoir to provide them with water pressure. Typically, the reservoir water level would drop low enough by midafternoon that the steam-driven Canal Street pumps would again begin moving water from the holding cistern by the river to the reservoir up the hill to replenish the water supply while also supplying water pressure to downtown Lafayette homes and businesses directly. With the threat that the boiler's coal fires at the pump station would soon be extinguished by the rising floodwater, the water that was already in Columbian Park Reservoir was the only source of drinkable water for Lafayette. In addition to supplying drinking water, the Columbian Park Reservoir provided the water that was used to fight fires. With the Canal Street waterworks unable to replenish the reservoir and the flood continuing unabated, Superintendent Camardy predicted that if the citizens didn't significantly curb their water use, "there will not be a drop of water in the city mains by day after tomorrow, and the city will be left without fire protection."[96]

NO LIGHT, NO HEAT

Not only was water unable to be pumped to the reservoir, but by Tuesday evening, the Merchants Electric Light Association Plant, which supplied much of the power to Lafayette, was inundated by the floodwater, owing to its relatively close location to the river on lower ground near the foot of the Brown Street Bridge. With no way to keep the boilers lit to provide steam for the pumps that drove the electricity-generating dynamos, power was cut off late Tuesday night, leaving only the much smaller Fort Wayne and Northern Indiana Traction Company's powerhouse to supply electricity for lighting in downtown Lafayette. This smaller powerhouse was located near the east end of the railroad bridge on the Lafayette side of the river, and it had originally been built to just supply electricity for the Fort Wayne and Northern Indiana Traction Company's electric railcars that ran within Lafayette and West Lafayette. But in 1908, the traction company saw the profit potential from generating greater amounts of electricity beyond the needs of the rail line and invested $50,000 to upgrade the plant to a 2,200-horsepower plant capable of supplying enough electricity for the electric car lines within Lafayette, for much of the rail line between Lafayette and Logansport and for some of the downtown Lafayette area. With the shutdown of the larger Merchants Electric Light Association Plant due to the flood, Lafayette's sole source of electricity and electrical light was this much smaller power plant. Unfortunately, like the Merchants Association's plant, the Fort Wayne and Northern Indiana Traction Company's twin smokestack powerhouse was at risk because it was nestled far too close to the flooding Wabash River.[97]

At 10:00 p.m. on Tuesday, the *Lafayette Morning Journal* reported that the workers at the traction company's powerhouse were barely holding the floodwater at bay, using the coal that was normally used to heat the boilers to form a makeshift dam against the rising water. Unfortunately, the coal dam was permeable, and the force of the water meant that a constant and growing stream of water continued to pour into the building. Four pumps that were located within pits in the powerhouse were barely keeping the floodwater levels inside the building low enough to allow the powerhouse's operations to continue. Not only was there a threat of water from around the powerhouse coming in through the coal dam, but also, river water was pushing into the building through sewer and water drains, the water pressure easily lifting the heavy steel manhole covers off the drainpipes located around the powerhouse. To keep the manhole covers in place and reduce the

A photograph of the interior the Fort Wayne and Northern Indiana Traction Company's powerhouse at the foot of the railroad bridge in Lafayette. Steam pumps drove the huge piston rods that can be seen connected to the flywheel on the right. A belt from the flywheel ran to the electrical dynamo on the left to generate the electricity to power the streetcars that ran downtown and on the spur line between West Lafayette and Battleground. *From the Pete Bill collection.*

geyser of floodwater from pushing upward and into the building, workers loaded 150,000 pounds of sand on top of the covers. The *Lafayette Morning Journal* quoted Superintendent Jack Abbott as saying, "We are now holding our own, but the water is coming in faster and faster. We hope to last through the night but make no promises for tomorrow."[98]

The supply of gas was also in jeopardy. The production of flammable gas by the Indiana Lighting Company in Lafayette and piped to West Lafayette through large gas pipelines running across the Main Street Bridge was ordered to be shut down at 9:00 p.m. on Tuesday evening for fear that the gas main would rupture if the Main Street Bridge collapsed. As of Tuesday night, West Lafayette was cut off from gas for lighting. The flood deepened around the Indiana Lighting Company all through Tuesday evening and into night, and at 3:30 a.m. on Wednesday, the *Lafayette Morning Journal* received word that the floodwater had made it impossible to keep

When the floodwaters extinguished the Merchants Electric Light Association's boilers, the dynamos of the smaller Fort Wayne and Northern Indiana Traction Company powerhouse provided the only source of electricity for Lafayette. Fortunately, in 1908, the company had increased the electrical generating capacity of the dynamos so they could provide electricity to areas of downtown Lafayette. As the floodwaters came in under the doors and up through the manhole covers in the floor, the flood threatened to extinguish the boilers that powered the pumps for these dynamos, terminating any remaining electricity production for the city. *From the Pete Bill collection.*

Lafayette's North Ninth Street, near Greenbush Street and Greenbush Cemetery. The flood extended east, across Ninth Street, to the edge of the cemetery, but it never invaded the cemetery itself. *From the postcard collection of Arnold L. Sweet.*

the gas-producing engines going. Without any new gas being pumped into Tippecanoe County, the community was totally dependent on the volume of gas that was contained in its two large gas reservoir tanks. The utility estimated that the supply of gas for lighting, cooking and heating would be exhausted by noon on Wednesday.[99]

In mid-March 1913, during the week of the flood, the weather was still cold, and snow was lying heavily on top of the frozen ground and structures. While wood-burning stoves and fireplaces still provided heat in some homes, coal and coal-oil furnaces and boilers had become more widely used after the turn of the century in Tippecanoe County. Thus, heat for homes and buildings relied heavily on coal and coal oil for either direct heat or for heating boilers that, in turn, provided steam or hot water for heat. Unfortunately, with Amos Mustard's coal barn at the West Lafayette Coal Company submerged, one of the main sources of coal for the west side was no longer available, meaning that heating in the cold mid-March weather of 1913 would have to come from whatever supply of coal and oil homeowners had on hand.

FAR-REACHING EFFECTS OF TUESDAY'S RISING FLOOD

People were not the only living things affected by the encroaching water. Horses, cattle and other livestock animals were reported to have been wandering loose around downtown Lafayette at the peak of the flood late Tuesday. The La Fayette Union Stock Yard, which was located south of downtown Lafayette at First and William Streets and just three hundred feet from the banks of the Wabash River, was filled with animals in holding pens as the floodwaters reached it on Tuesday afternoon. Without an option of being able to relocate the livestock to higher ground in any organized manner, the animals were quickly branded for identification and then turned loose to fend for themselves against the floodwaters. The nearby neighborhood likely had a parade of livestock wandering through the streets and yards in search of higher ground. Numerous other businesses in downtown Lafayette also had horses or pens for livestock because, in 1913, horse-drawn wagons were still the primary means by which goods and equipment were delivered throughout town. The Lafayette Artificial Ice Company and the Sanitary Milk Company, both of which relied heavily on horse-drawn wagons, had to move all of their horses from the encroaching flood and find stalls farther away from the river on higher ground in Lafayette. Indeed, an exodus of animals and livestock from riverside businesses was likely seen all day Tuesday as the floodwaters rose.[100]

By Tuesday evening, the huge Thieme and Wagner Brewery, which was located not far from the east bank of the Wabash River at the junction of Fourth and Union Streets, had floodwater running through the plant as the flood crept up to Fourth Street and began working its way farther into downtown Lafayette. The *Lafayette Daily Courier* reported that water was "tearing through the Born Ice Plant" located near the eastern end of the railroad bridge. The inundation suffered by the Thieme and Wagner Brewery and the Born Ice Plant were shared by all Lafayette businesses that were located within three or four blocks of the river as their basements and lower floors filled with the icy floodwater. Armies of workers and citizens swarmed both the businesses and residences to remove people, equipment and valuable inventory as the water rose. With the rising water came the fear of electrocution, as the water was beginning to encroach on the electrical outlets and sockets of those businesses, some of which were still receiving electricity. This further prompted immediate evacuation. By Tuesday afternoon, all business operations between Lafayette's Third Street and the river had ceased.[101] By Tuesday evening, many of these businesses' owners feared that their battles with the rising water were lost.

As night settled on the river communities in Tippecanoe County, the rain began to fall again, and the Wabash River continued to rise.

Chapter 5

THE DESTRUCTION PEAKS

Wednesday, March 26, 1913

It had rained all Tuesday night and into Wednesday morning, and water was pouring into the tributaries upstream from Tippecanoe County, pushing a rising wave of water down the Wabash River toward Lafayette. By Wednesday morning, the river level had already exceeded the flood levels attained by what was referred to in the newspapers as the Great Flood of 1883. Hydrologists would later estimate that the volume of deep and turbulent floodwater flowing in the narrow gap between Lafayette and West Lafayette on March 26 was more than 190,000 cubic feet of water per second. By comparison, the flow of water over the combination of the Canadian Horseshoe Falls, the American Falls and the Bridal Veil Falls that constitute all of Niagara Falls averages only 100,300 cubic feet per second, about half the volume of the flooded Wabash River on March 26. The enormity of the volume of the thirty-foot-deep water passing through the relatively narrow space between Lafayette and West Lafayette gives an idea of the massive destructive force exerted by the Wabash floodwater against any obstacles, natural or man-made, that stood in its path.

During the darkness of Tuesday night and early Wednesday morning, huge booming, splintering crashes were heard periodically coming from the river. The *Lafayette Morning Journal* reported that, at 11:00 p.m. on Tuesday evening, a thundering crash was heard at the west end of the Main Street Bridge that convinced the crowds who were still gathered on the east bank that the bridge had gone down. With little electricity available to much of

This photograph shows two houseboats that had broken loose from their moorings and, because of the high water, had become trapped against the railroad bridge until the force of the current either shoved them under the bridge or broke them apart. *From the postcard collection of Arnold L. Sweet.*

the city and with only a few lanterns to illuminate the night, it could not be determined if the bridges were still standing. The question of the fate of the Main Street Bridge would have to wait until dawn.[102]

Stories that were published in the newspapers described how, on this Tuesday night, strange lights were seen floating down the river, perhaps coming from a lit lantern that was caught in the debris of a swept-away barn, shed or house. No one could ever verify the source of the lights on the river, but with the darkness of the night and the sound of debris crashing against the bridges, the bobbing lights seemed eerie.[103]

When dawn finally broke on Wednesday, March 26, the Wabash River had been above the eleven-foot flood stage for almost two days, and it was still rising. Overnight temperatures had dropped, and in the gray morning light, snow was falling in earnest, eventually depositing six inches of accumulation on the debris, the remaining ironwork of the Brown Street Bridge and the roofs of partially submerged houses and buildings.[104] The morning light also revealed that the predictions that the Main Street Bridge would collapse and the railroad embankment would give way to the floodwater were incorrect. Both remained standing.

The *Lafayette Morning Journal* had surprisingly little information about local events, and its front page focused instead on the impact of the flood in Indianapolis and other communities in central Indiana. Newspapers may have focused more on national news because all of the local telephone and telegraph lines were still down and all lines out of Lafayette had been severed except for the single wire to Indianapolis, thus isolating Lafayette from all outside communication save news coming from Indianapolis.[105] An article in the *Journal* cited the need for relief to assist the victims of tornado-stricken Terre Haute, and another provided more details about the tornadic destruction in Omaha, Nebraska. Early reports of flood-related destruction due to breached dams or levees in Ohio contained dramatic descriptions of destruction and life-and-death struggles against the sudden floods in Springfield and Dayton. According to the *Lafayette Morning Journal*, people in Dayton, Ohio, were "dying like rats in their homes, bodies [were] washing around in the streets, and no relief in sight." Estimates were made that said over 30,000 people were homeless and that 540 people were killed in the Dayton, Ohio area alone.[106] As would be noted in news accounts published later that lamented the yellow-press sensationalism in the early flood reporting, the initial estimates of deaths and homelessness were often heavily exaggerated but nonetheless reported by newspapers as spectacular facts.

Locally, the Wednesday edition of the *Lafayette Morning Journal* reported that the Wabash River was still rising at a rate of six inches an hour and that a surge of water rose six inches from 9:45 p.m. to 10:00 p.m. Tuesday evening as measured on the wall of the Ydrad Boat Clubhouse at the east end of the Main Street Bridge.[107] Another direct measurement between 9:40 p.m. and 11:00 p.m. reported that the water had risen eleven inches in a little over an hour.[108]

The Bridges Are Still There, For Now

The railroad bridge and embankment had held overnight. After the Lake Erie and Western special train delivered marooned west siders across the railroad bridge to West Lafayette on Tuesday evening, officials with the New York Central System decided to move Chicago, Terre Haute and Southeastern Railway coal cars, which were loaded with an estimated thirty-seven thousand tons of coal, onto the bridge and south tracks of the embankment to exert a downward force to keep the floodwaters from lifting the bridge decking off of the piers and to help stabilize the embankment. Because the railroad embankment was composed of timbers buried in earth, the flood current flowing by the base of the embankment was washing away the supporting dirt. By Wednesday morning, the floodwaters had eroded so much of the upstream, northern-facing side of the embankment that fifty feet of the northern track dangled unsupported in the air over the eroded embankment held up only by the embankment remaining under the south track. Farther west of that point, closer to River Road, the floodwater had softened the embankment, allowing the northern track to settle about three feet.

Starting Tuesday afternoon and continuing into Wednesday, volunteers and railroad workers were recruited to fill bags with sand from a nearby gravel pit and load the sandbags along with heavy gravel, small boulders, coal, railroad ties and discarded tires onto flatbed railcars, which were pushed back toward the bridge on the intact southern rail track. Once positioned next to the north-facing embankment erosion site, volunteers threw the sandbags and gravel, along with the other materials from the railcars, down the embankment's north face in an attempt to reinforce the embankment and lessen the rate of erosion from the floodwater.[109]

Still, the continually rising water meant that, eventually, the flood would likely destroy both the railroad bridge and west side embankment leading to it. By Wednesday morning, engineers were proposing plans to save the

This photograph, taken from atop the Tippecanoe County Courthouse, shows white crests of frothy, turbulent water along the Big Four bridge spans and the railroad embankment conveying the tremendous force of water that these structures resisted. *From the postcard collection of Arnold L. Sweet.*

This close-up of the Big Four Railroad embankment shows a group of men throwing gravel, boulders and timbers from atop loaded railcars down the embankment's north face to reinforce the embankment and slow the erosion caused by the turbulent current. By the time the flood had peaked, the embankment had eroded from under the northern set of tracks, leaving them suspended in air. *From the postcard collection of Arnold L. Sweet.*

railroad bridge by destroying the embankment with dynamite to reduce the bottleneck the railroad embankment caused to the flood flow. By opening up the space and allowing a wider and easier southward flow of the river, the force of the floodwater against the railroad bridge's piers and abutments would be decreased and increase the chances for the bridge's survival. A measurement of the rails at the east end of the bridge at Lafayette's South Street revealed that the combined force of the floodwater and the debris impacting the railway bridge had moved the bridge rails five inches out of alignment with the anchored tracks on the Lafayette riverbank, preventing any safe movement of railcars or locomotives across the bridge.[110]

Although the Main Street Bridge was still standing by Wednesday morning, the tilt to the bridge deck that had been noticed the day before had further increased. Either because the floodwater had risen in the previous twenty-four hours or the second stone pier from the west had sunk deeper into the riverbed, the stone bridge pier was by then completely covered by the flowing water, leading observers to speculate that the pier may have been washed away. It was later revealed that the pier was still present, but its base was sinking into river. The year before the flood, in 1912, the Main Street Bridge piers had been widened with the construction of an additional pier beside the north (upstream) side of the original pier to provide stronger support for the Fort Wayne and Northern Indiana streetcar track that ran along the north side of the bridge decking.

At the peak of the flood, the Wabash River was even with the underside of the Big Four Railroad Bridge spans. The fully loaded coal cars had been moved onto the bridge to exert downward pressure to keep the floodwater from sweeping the spans off of their stone bridge piers. *From the postcard collection of Arnold L. Sweet.*

The streetcar rails, which were installed shortly after the construction of the bridge, were mounted on an extension from the bridge's original decking. However, with newer and heavier streetcars crossing the bridge, the decking extension was considered inadequate to support the heavier cars, necessitating additional support from the stone pier widening. On Wednesday, March 26, however, the disappearance of the original stone pier below the turbulent surface of the river led some observers to speculate that the entire weight of the sagging two bridge spans then rested solely on the narrower recent addition to the second pier.[111] As later investigations of the riverbed and the pier revealed, the widening of the pier by the addition of the track-supporting pier in 1912 changed the dynamics of the water flow around the pier, creating a back eddy on the downstream side of the original pier. The tremendous volume of floodwater being forced through the narrows between the abutments on either side of the Main Street Bridge accelerated the water past the foot of the bridge piers and exacerbated the eddy's scouring of the river bottom, resulting in removal of thousands of cubic feet of riverbed around the pier base and allowing the older pier to sink more than a foot. With the sinking of the pier, gravity provided the force needed to tilt the two spans of the bridge toward the river and twist the steel superstructure of the bridge.[112]

The Main Street Bridge on Thursday, March 27, 1913, at the height of the 1913 flood. The sag of the bridge over the sinking pier illustrates why many predicted that the Main Street Bridge, like the Brown Street Bridge, would fail "imminently." *From the postcard collection of Arnold L. Sweet.*

The sinking of the pier on which the the Main Street Bridge rested not only allowed gravity to twist the bridge's ironwork but also allowed it to damage the utility lines that were carried by the bridge. At 9:00 p.m. on Tuesday, March 25, the Indiana Lighting Company shut off the gas line that was carried under the bridge for fear of a gas fire or explosion should the bridge collapse. *From the postcard collection of Arnold L. Sweet.*

Meanwhile, the Fort Wayne and Northern Indiana Traction Company power plant at the foot of railroad bridge at South Street had somehow made it through the night against the rising water around the building and was still producing some electricity. The combination of water pumps working at full capacity, the makeshift coal dam around the plant and the tons of sand dumped on top of the manhole covers to keep the drainpipes from shooting geysers of floodwater into the station were barely keeping the incoming water at bay. With the Wabash River still rising, Superintendent Jack Abbott was uncertain how much longer the boilers could remain lit to drive the electricity-producing dynamos of this last operating public utility. Although electric streetlamps were not lit in an effort to conserve the limited electricity available, other businesses in the immediate downtown area did have some supply of electricity to run equipment or operate telephone or telegraph lines for communication.

THE CITY COULD GO UP IN FLAMES

Without the ability to operate the boilers that drove the huge water pumps, the Lafayette Pumping Station was still unable to pump water to replenish the dwindling supply of fresh water at the Columbian Park Reservoir. The water supply in the reservoir was described Wednesday morning as being "low and constantly diminishing." The local newspaper and Lafayette mayor George Durgan urged each citizen to act as "a committee of one" to take extraordinary measures to prevent any conflagration from starting, since the lack of water meant any significant fire could not have been extinguished. In his proclamation, the mayor voiced concern about the fire risk created by the increased use of wood- or coal-burning stoves for heating and cooking and the widespread use of open flames from candles or oil lamps for light since so many no longer had illuminating gas or electricity for light.[113] Indeed, the combination of having many older, wood-framed factory or warehouse buildings crowded together with livery stables loaded with dried hay and straw meant that downtown Lafayette in 1913 was a monumentally destructive fire waiting to happen. With no efficient way to bring water to a fire, downtown Lafayette was a flooded tinderbox still capable of bursting into flames from a single poorly located stove, open flame, toppled candle or tipped lantern.

The fears for a potentially devastating fire almost came true on the morning of Wednesday, March 27, in an unexpected way. As of Wednesday morning, the large Thieme and Wagner Brewery at the corner of Fourth and Union Streets was on the edge of the rising floodwater. Stored in the yard next to the large brick-faced brewery were barrels of lime, which were used in the commercial brewing process. Lime is a reactive substance, and when combined with water, it becomes "slaked" lime via a chemical process that can generate enough heat to ignite combustible materials. Thus, when the floodwaters began to infiltrate the yard that was filled with wooden barrels of lime, enough chemical heat was generated to set the barrels on fire. Although the Lafayette Fire Department still had enough water pressure to fight the blaze, pouring water onto the lime only increased the heat-producing reaction, igniting adjoining barrels and the shed in which the lime barrels were stored. The only course of action was to extinguish the wood as it ignited, knowing that the chemical heat would reignite any wood not kept wet. The firefighters found themselves wading through water that was described by the *Lafayette Morning Journal* as being shoulder high in places and icy cold. The effort of working in the icy floodwater and cold weather conditions must have been physically exhausting. Captain C.O. Johnson was overcome by the cold and exertion and collapsed under the

The Thieme and Wagner Brewery was a prominent feature on downtown Lafayette's near north side at the western terminus of Union Street at North Fourth Street. Its location was close to the river, which can be seen in this image to the right, behind the buildings. *From the postcard collection of Arnold L. Sweet.*

Thieme and Wagner Brewery, looking northward along Fourth Street. The floodwaters invaded a building that held several barrels of lime used as an alkalinizing agent in the brewing process. Because this form of lime reacts violently when mixed with water, the floodwater caused the lime barrels to generate enough heat to ignite the barrels, threatening the entire brewery. *From the postcard collection of Arnold L. Sweet.*

water. Fortunately, he was quickly rescued and transported to St. Elizabeth Hospital, where he recovered. The firefighters persisted in containing the fire whenever the wood burst into flames, and eventually, the chemical process literally burned itself out.[114]

Although Lafayette's water crisis was well publicized in the local paper, West Lafayette's water situation was no less dire. The smaller pumping station on the west side that pushed water up to the steel storage tank at the top of the hill at Grant and Salisbury Streets had ceased its operations on Tuesday. In contrast to the large reservoir at Columbian Park that supplied Lafayette, the West Lafayette reservoir tank that still stands today in what is now Grand View Cemetery was a much smaller reservoir and was rapidly being depleted of water. Like Lafayette, West Lafayette would soon be depleted of any fresh water for personal use or for fighting fires if citizens didn't immediately take action to conserve water use from their taps.

Not only were people in the two riverside communities cut off from physically reaching each other, but wire communications across the river were also disrupted by the loss of the Brown Street Bridge and damage to the Main Street Bridge. This loss of communication across the river was compounded by the damage to telegraph and telephone lines throughout the city and county caused by the previous weekend's gales. The sagging of the Main Street Bridge snapped the main telephone cable for the Lafayette Telephone Company, which ran along the bottom of the bridge, cutting off the majority of phone communication between the two cities. In contrast, the Bell System ran a single line over the top of the Main Street Bridge, and in spite of the twisting of the ironworks, this line remained intact, allowing some limited telephone contact between the two sides and with the rest of the world.

As would be expected, the disruption of wagon and rail traffic across the bridges meant that food and other supplies were cut off from some areas of Tippecanoe County. By Tuesday, when the rising waters began to lap at the doors of grocers in the west side levee area, all inventory was moved to other grocers or locations farther away from the flooding river. Charlie's Bakery at 124 East State Street, which was located higher up on the Chauncey Hill, was able to supply bread early Wednesday morning and had another batch for sale at noon. But without any fresh water, no more bread was able to be made and he closed his shop.[115] The *Lafayette Morning Journal* reported that by mid-morning Wednesday, all grocery stores on the west side would be closed, but merchants promised to fill the orders they had previously received as long as supplies held out.[116] With no milk or bread, the boardinghouses and student dormitories on Purdue's campus had little, if anything, for food. With west side citizens and grocers cut off from Lafayette and their usual sources of produce and foodstuffs, a growing sense of fear about a potential impending famine began to circulate in the community. The local newspapers reported that those west side citizens who had automobiles were traveling into the country and smaller surrounding farm communities in search of sources for coal oil, eggs, milk and butter.[117]

In addition to coal being unavailable because of the flooding of the West Lafayette Coal Company, coal oil for heating against the cold weather was also no longer available anywhere on the west side. The west side grocers pooled their resources and ordered a large tank of coal oil from a supplier in Brookston to replenish the dwindling supply. However, the Monon tracks north of Lafayette and the Monon railyards on Lafayette's northside were underwater from the flooded Wildcat Creek and Wabash River; therefore, no railcar from Brookston could get the coal oil any closer to West Lafayette than Battleground.[118] Realizing that rail shipment was not an option, the coal oil supplier hitched up a four-horse team and slowly pulled a wagon with the coal oil tank from Brookston down the muddy roads to West Lafayette. It was hoped that by taking the roads north of West Lafayette and west of Brookston, the wagon could avoid any washed-out river or creek bridges and arrive in West Lafayette on Thursday morning.[119]

Although West Side High School had closed because it had no available water to fill the boilers and heat the school, the other public schools remained open because they were heated by flame-heated air and were not dependent on a water supply. Purdue University continued to have water for its boiler heat by using the water from its swimming pool to fill the boilers.[120]

The River Brings Dead Animals

Throughout Wednesday, reports continued to circulate of many unusual and bizarre things carried down the Wabash River or found floating in the adjacent flooded areas. The force of the floodwater had shoved the ironwork from the collapsed Brown Street Bridge span downstream toward the Main Street Bridge, while other parts of tangled steel were observed sticking out of the water as far south as the railroad bridge.[121] A pile of debris served as a makeshift raft for two live rabbits and a chicken that sailed by Lafayette among the floating boards, branches and parts of wood-framed barns, sheds and houses. Shortly before noon on Wednesday, the remnants of the Wallace Circus, which had been housed for the winter in Peru, Indiana, fifty-five miles upstream on the Wabash River, came floating by. Brightly colored fabric, stained by mud and debris, was mixed with wagons and the floating bodies of dead animals. Upstream in Peru, the devastation of the winter circus grounds caused by the rapid rise of the Wabash flowing through the city had resulted in the deaths of dozens of circus animals, ranging from large cats like lions and tigers to elephants. In the subsequent days, as the floodwaters in Peru receded, animal carcasses were uncovered throughout the city. It is unknown how many other animals floated downstream toward Lafayette and Terre Haute, mixed in among the rest of the flood debris that passed by from as far away as Fort Wayne.[122]

The predominantly Irish neighborhood south of Main Street in Lafayette, near the Dryfus Packing Plant and St. Ann's Catholic Church, was referred to colloquially as "Connorsville," as there was a relatively large number of

O'Connor families living in the area. The *Lafayette Daily Courier* reported that, by Wednesday afternoon, the Connorsville area was "totally underwater," with the majority of homes submerged or lifted from their foundations and swept away in the torrent. Not all the residents of Connorsville had left their flooded homes, and with the rising water, the ones who had not fled were then trapped in their homes. The city and the police department commandeered the shallow-draft boats that were normally used for leisurely rides on the Columbian Park pond and used them instead to move stranded people from their inundated homes to safer ground.[123] It was reported that Captain James O'Connor moved his family from his rapidly flooding house to his riverboat, the *General DeHart*. Unlike the fate of many other houseboats and watercraft that had been ripped from their moorings and dashed against the Main Street Bridge or railroad bridges, Captain O'Connor had wisely removed the *General DeHart*'s mooring lines from the wooden pilings on the east bank and had instead anchored the lines to a large building in the nearby flooded stockyards. With the *General DeHart* securely held in place, the O'Connor family had a very close and firsthand view of the raging Wabash River and the flood.

By Wednesday, March 26, the Wabash River had already flooded the predominantly Irish south Lafayette neighborhood of "Connorsville," inundating the Lafayette Box Board and Paper Company (the "Strawboard Works"), covering Sycamore Street in the foreground and surrounding St. Ann's Church (*left side*). The church survived the 1913 flood and still stands today. *From the postcard collection of Arnold L. Sweet.*

The Dryfus Packing and Provision Company on the Lafayette's south side near the river was founded by Leopold and Ferdinand Dryfus in 1887 and could process up to three hundred hogs and head of cattle per day. When the flood inundated the holding pens, the animals were turned loose and roamed the south side and downtown Lafayette for several days. *From the postcard collection of Arnold L. Sweet.*

Back on the west side, by Wednesday afternoon the lowland between the Main Street Levee and the railroad embankment had been mostly scoured clean of timber-framed buildings. Of the dozens of buildings and structures located in the lowland, including the expansive wooden barns and stables of the Lafayette Transfer Company, only two significantly sized buildings remained: the Lafayette Fence and Machine Company building and the Esterline Company building. Both buildings were constructed of block and concrete and were thus more securely rooted to their foundations. As the sun set late on Wednesday, only the top of the long Esterline building could be seen above the water.[124]

Buildings perched along the relatively higher Main Street Levee were not necessarily protected from the impact of the floodwater because their foundations often rested six feet below the grade of the levee on the floor of the basin of the Chauncey Bottomlands. Although it was invisible to observers during the peak of the flood, the force of the floodwater that had poured southward across the Brown Street Levee and cascaded over the Main Street Levee at the low point near the Morgan and Torrenga garage had scoured out dirt from around the foundations of several buildings lining Main Street, leaving the buildings teetering at odd angles, or had caused the foundations of others to crumble completely. Paved sidewalks

The submerged Chauncey Bottomlands between the Main Street Levee (*to the left*) and the railroad embankment (*out of the picture, to the right*). The arched roof of the submerged long cinder-block building is the Esterline Company's building. It was one of the few buildings left standing in the bottomlands after the flood. *From the postcard collection of Arnold L. Sweet.*

South River Road (Ellsworth Road) in West Lafayette, looking north from atop the Big Four embankment's bridge. By Thursday, March 27, the floodwater, which had previously covered the road, was just starting to recede. The flooded expanse to the right in this image is the Chauncey Bottomlands, which was swept clean of almost all its buildings. *From the postcard collection of Arnold L. Sweet.*

Floodwater pours across the Main Street Levee and into the Chauncey Bottomlands basin, eroding the levee and gouging huge craters from around the foundations of buildings. This hole around an automobile repair shop near Ellsworth Road was more than ten feet deep. *From the postcard collection of Arnold L. Sweet.*

along the levee and road surfaces were torn up and swept away, and the steel rails of the streetcar traction company along the levee were twisted into curving spirals.

Even if they had not been physically swept away, most of the buildings lining the high ground along the Main Street Levee were irreparably damaged. As previously described, many of the wooden structures closest to the river simply floated off their foundations and were dashed against the railroad bridge. One of the last buildings along the Main Street Levee to be picked up by the torrent was the veterinary infirmary belonging to Dr. Funkhouser and Dr. Whitesell. Dr. Whitesell was the person who had heroically rescued Burkhouse and Wangerin after the collapse of the Brown Street Bridge. In spite of attempts to protect the infirmary located along Main Street, at 5:00 p.m., the water lifted the building off of its foundation, floated it out to the main channel of the river. With a great velocity, the river smashed it to splinters against the railroad bridge.[125] At the time, the whereabouts of Dr. Whitesell were unknown and gave rise to concerns that he may have been lost with the building. Fortunately, it was later reported by the *Lafayette Morning Journal* on March 29 that the "missing" Dr. Whitesell had been "found" when he came to Lafayette from the west side to procure supplies.[126] Prior to the infirmary being swept away, a valuable beagle hound had been taken to the veterinary infirmary for treatment the week before the flood and was still housed there when the floodwaters began lapping at the building's edge. As the floodwaters began to flow into the first floor of the infirmary, the dog was relocated to the second floor of the building. However, when the building unexpectedly lifted off its foundation and smashed against the railroad bridge, it was presumed the dog had died. On Thursday, the dog's owner was walking over the railroad levee when he saw a man with a dog the man claimed he had rescued from driftwood along the riverbanks. The dog turned out to be the missing, and presumed dead, beagle hound. How the dog escaped from the infirmary and survived is a mystery.[127] With the veterinary infirmary destroyed, the *Lafayette Morning Journal* directed readers to reach Dr. Whitesell at the Carson Drugstore in West Lafayette and his partner, Dr. Funkhouser, at Bartlett's Drugstore in Lafayette.[128]

By Wednesday evening, the circumstances surrounding the lack of food, drinkable water, electricity and gas had not improved for the west siders. By 5:00 p.m., the water supply in the large steel tank at the top of the hill at Grant and Salisbury Streets had been exhausted, forcing citizens to get their water from individual residential water cisterns that were often constructed alongside urban homes in the 1800s and other small reservoirs of stored water throughout the community. A hurriedly assembled meeting of West Lafayette citizens listened to Everett Vawter, the community leader and civil engineer whose Lafayette Bridge Company had constructed the Main Street Bridge, explain the dire circumstances the community was facing. With little to no coal available on the west side, Purdue president Stone pledged to move some of the university's coal supply onto a railcar at the university's powerhouse for local citizens to purchase in small amounts.[129]

THE PRESSES KEPT RUNNING...

Like all the other businesses in Lafayette, by Wednesday evening, Lafayette's newspapers, the *Morning Journal* and the *Daily Courier*, were both struggling to continue operations, supply printed papers and keep the county informed of critical information. With telegraph and telephone communication almost completely shut down, the newspapers were the only means by which information could be disseminated to Tippecanoe

County. Communities were so dependent on the newspaper that one citizen of Battleground literally risked his life to navigate his boat downstream to Lafayette, pick up several Lafayette newspapers and slowly make his way back upstream to distribute them to the Battleground community. The small amount of electricity generated by the Fort Wayne and Northern Indiana Traction Company power plant supplied the light needed inside the newspaper press rooms to set type and continue operations. However, candles and lamps were scrounged up in anticipation of losing electricity during the overnight typesetting for the morning edition of the paper. Oil stoves were pressed into use to keep the temperatures in the building high enough to help keep the mechanical presses operating and, just as importantly, to keep the machine operators warm enough to perform their tasks. The presses were driven by an electrical motor, and in anticipating the eventual loss of electricity should the Traction Line Powerhouse have failed, the *Journal* switched to a gas-powered engine. The linotype machines that were used by the newspapers to set type in 1913 were dependent on gas or other sources of heat to melt a combination of lead, antimony and tin into a liquid state that was then pushed into molds made by the operator for each line of newspaper type (hence the name of the machine, "line-of-type"). By 1913, the linotype machines had, for twenty years, mostly replaced the slower and more tedious process of selecting and placing individual letter keys into a frame that would then be used by the press to create a page of newspaper. By Wednesday, March 26, the city's gas supply was exhausted. Faced with a morning deadline, the *Lafayette Morning Journal* printers were required to set the entire paper overnight by selecting and mounting the individual pieces of print type by hand. Fortunately, the *Journal* had saved the old drawer cases of individual letter print blocks for just such an emergency and were able to produce an abbreviated version of the morning newspaper, complete with the occasional mistakes and inverted letters characteristic of the old method of printing.[130] The next day, the afternoon newspaper, the *Lafayette Daily Courier*, reported a similar challenging tale of having to not only set the paper by hand but also print an additional five thousand "Extra" editions for the citizens who were hungry for information.[131]

By Wednesday evening, the floodwater had crept twenty feet up State Street Hill in West Lafayette, and every home on the Wabash River side of Ellsworth Road was flooded halfway up the first-floor doors and windows.[132] Because of their higher elevations, the homes on the other side of this road had not yet been touched by the floodwater. But as night settled and the view of the river's flood edge disappeared into the evening gloom, the fear was that by morning, the flood would reach into all of these homes as well.

At 10:00 p.m. on Wednesday, March 26, some welcome news finally arrived. The flooded Wabash River, as measured by the station at the Brown Street Measuring Station, had stopped rising. The crest of the flood was measured at just under thirty-three feet, a full thirty feet higher than the river measured just four days before on Saturday, March 22.

Chapter 6

THE WATER BEGINS TO RECEDE, THE DAMAGE IS REVEALED

Thursday, March 27, 1913

At 1:00 a.m. on Thursday, March 27, the Wabash River started to recede.[133] At its highest level, the thirty-three-foot flood crest had pushed river water twenty feet up State Street Hill. River Road was underwater, and the floodwater cascaded underneath the arched New York Central System Railroad bridge over River Road, scouring out the road and the surrounding ground on the other side of the arch.[134] However, without any additional rain or significant snow upstream in the Wabash River watershed during the previous twenty-four hours, the water levels in Tippecanoe County began to fall almost as rapidly as they had risen. On Thursday morning, the river gauge at the Lafayette Box Board and Paper Company, located on Chestnut Street in the Connorsville area of south Lafayette, reported that the water was falling at the rate of two inches per hour. At the Harry B. Lyman Coal Company on Second Street in Lafayette, the river gauge indicated that the water had dropped a foot between midnight and mid-morning on Thursday and was continuing to fall quickly.[135]

By Thursday morning, Superintendent Jack Abbott, who had been battling to keep the Fort Wayne and Northern Indiana Traction Company Power Station at South Street going in spite of floodwater surrounding the building, proclaimed of the flood, "It looks like we have beaten it out." The rising water had crept up to the door of the engine room, which contained the machinery that drove the dynamos providing the only electrical power to Lafayette. But it wasn't until the river had started to recede that the engine room was declared safe and some assurance was given that electrical power would continue to be generated. The *Lafayette Daily Courier* lauded Abbott's efforts with the headline "Hero Beats the Flood."[136]

With the falling water, the damage assessment could begin as structures—or missing structures—were uncovered. The north side of the railroad embankment, for three hundred feet beyond the west end of the railroad bridge, had been partially washed out, leaving the northern set of the two tracks hanging suspended over the gap. The boulders and materials that had been thrown down the north embankment face during the previous two days likely prevented the embankment from collapsing completely. However, on Thursday, the floodwater was still several feet above flood stage, and the current continued to hammer away at the embankment, eroding the dirt and threatening to collapse the railroad embankment. Crews continued to heave large loads of gravel, rocks and railroad ties onto the north face of the embankment throughout Thursday. In contrast to the north track, the engineers of the New York Central System pronounced the south track to be as "solid as a rock."[137] The reported malalignment of the rails between the east end of the railroad bridge and the Lafayette riverbank noted on Wednesday was confirmed on Thursday during the track inspection. But while the New York Central System Bridge's steel superstructure had been pushed out of alignment by the unrelenting impacts of floating buildings and debris, the stone piers on which the bridge rested were reported by the *Lafayette Daily Courier* to be "as solid and straight as ever."[138] Superintendent C.C. Arnold of the Lake Erie and Western Railroad estimated that it would be two to three days before repairs could be made to the bridge sufficient to allow rail traffic to cross the bridge using the south set of tracks. The superintendent agreed with the newspaper's speculation that the bridge piers appeared to have escaped the flood undamaged; however, he stated that at least three hundred railcar loads of dirt would be needed to replace the part of the north side railroad embankment that had been lost to the flood's erosion.[139] In spite of the superintendent's prediction that resumption of rail traffic across the bridge would take a few days, others, like baker John B. Ruger, predicted a railcar with his bread products would be able to cross over to the west side on the Lake Erie and Western tracks "as early as Thursday evening."[140] As it turned out, the repairs went quickly, and the first regularly scheduled train to pass over the railroad bridge was the Big Four's Indianapolis-Chicago train that crossed the river on the southern rails around 8:00 a.m. on Friday.[141]

Wildcat Creek on Thursday, March 27. The force of the flood had ripped away the Fort Wayne and Northern Indiana Traction Company's trestle bridge, leaving steel rails twisted among the debris like limp strands of spaghetti. *Image courtesy of Tippecanoe County Historical Association.*

Like the New York Central System Railroad Bridge in Lafayette, the Monon Railroad Bridge over the abandoned Erie Canal at the north end of the Monon Shop Yards had been saved by parking heavily loaded coal railcars on the bridge to exert the downward force necessary to keep the bridge and rails securely atop the bridge's piers. With the Monon Bridge still intact, some rail traffic from Brookston, Chalmers, Monon and other points due north of Lafayette could resume on a limited basis.[142]

By noon on Thursday, the flooded Wildcat Creek, where, three days prior, the Rothenberger brothers had lost their lives, had receded enough that the creek was almost within its banks once again. The rapid drop allowed engineers to evaluate the Fort Wayne and Northern Indiana Traction Line (FW&NI) and the Lake Erie and Western tracks. Although multiple sections of the FW&NI traction line track had been washed away, the Lake Erie and Western Bridge and tracks had suffered minimal damage and were predicted to return to operation "very soon."[143]

West Side Supplies Begin to Trickle In

Gas and electricity were still not available to west siders as of Thursday morning, but in spite of that, the conditions on the west side had started to improve. As promised by Purdue University president Stone and Amos Mustard of the West Lafayette Coal Company, a railcar load of coal was delivered early Thursday morning to citizens of the west side. Cold west siders who were seeking some means to heat their homes lined up with wagons and carts to buy their allotted 250 to 500 pounds of coal at the cost of $1.25 per 500 pounds. By 9:00 a.m. on Thursday, ten tons of coal had been sold.[144] Around the same time that west siders were replenishing their coal supply, the four-horse team from Brookston arrived in West Lafayette hauling a large tank that contained three hundred gallons of coal oil. The oil was apportioned out in small quantities to individuals, providing some fuel for their furnaces.[145] Although these measures began to provide fuel for heating homes, the temperatures still dipped into the low twenties at night and only climbed to the low thirties during the day. Thus, coal or coal oil was used sparingly to keep homes and boardinghouses only slightly warmer than freezing. Without sufficient coal or coal oil to heat boiler water, which, in turn, provided heat to boardinghouses and Purdue classrooms, many Purdue students studied in bone-chilling cold rooms and often went to bed at sunset because of the lack of gas light or sources of heat.[146]

While some resources for providing heat were slowly coming back to both Lafayette and west side citizens, William Wallace of the Indiana Lighting Company announced that citizens would likely have to use candles for light and serve cold food for some time, as no gas would be produced until a detailed assessment of the flood damage to the gas-producing facility could be conducted. The *Lafayette Daily Courier* pessimistically reported that even if the gas manufacture resumed within a week, it could be as long as two weeks before citizens would have access to a reliable illuminating gas supply again.[147] This prediction didn't mention the additional challenges west siders faced due to the disruption of the gas line that was carried across the sagging Main Street Bridge and the time it would take to assess the damage and replace or repair the gas line.

In 1913, the lack of available gas negatively affected both gas light illumination and heating, but to a greater degree it halted gas cooking, which had become so widely used by 1913 that many households viewed the lack of gas for cooking as much of an inconvenience as the lack of water. On Thursday, the Indiana Lighting company warned that "possibly burners for cooking and illuminating purposes have been left open," presenting a risk for gas explosions from candles or lanterns whenever gas supply was restored, as homes could be filled with explosive gas through the open burners.[148] Without illuminating gas for light, the sudden demand for kerosene for lanterns exhausted kerosene oil supplies by Tuesday on the west side, and no more could be found "at any price."[149] The citizens on the Lafayette side of the river had a more ample supply of kerosene, and lit kerosene lanterns were soon seen in many buildings on the east side of the river. Because the water supply for fighting fires had not yet been replenished to either the Columbian Park Reservoir or the West Lafayette Water Tank by Friday, the risk for an accidental inferno from candle or kerosene lanterns was still very real, and citizens were warned once again to be very careful using any flame. Fortunately, by late Thursday afternoon, Wallace's inspection of the gas plant had been completed, and he reversed his dire prediction, announcing that, in "two days or so," the Indiana Lighting Company could begin manufacturing gas again to supply gas for lighting and cooking. By Saturday, March 29, a sufficient volume of gas had been generated and pushed into the mains so that households could once again use gas for heating, cooking and illumination, and the fire hazard from open candles and lit lanterns greatly diminished.[150]

Whereas the rising flood and the severed bridges and rail lines had prompted the newspapers to make dire predictions of a food famine in West Lafayette, a merchant from Otterbein reported at the Wednesday evening meeting that the Otterbein merchants were adequately stocked with provisions and would bring food and essential supplies to West Lafayette. As there was no significant waterway separating West Lafayette from Otterbein to impede the transport of goods, by early Thursday, west side merchants were receiving goods and provisions from Otterbein. Livestock owners in the rural northern and western parts of the county began harvesting livestock to resupply depleted west side grocers with fresh meat. The predicted food famine on the west side appeared to have been circumvented.

Like people, livestock in the affected communities also needed to be fed. Unlike today where livestock operations are separate from urban areas, in 1913 small farms were close to urban communities, and many townfolk had backyard poultry or small livestock. The Martin Feed Store, whose building was located on the south side of the Main Street Levee, was a central source for grain and hay. The Martin building, owned by John D. Martin, was one of the few buildings on the south side of the Main Street Levee that wasn't washed away or completely destroyed during the flood.

Unlike many of the buildings that lined the Main Street Levee that were washed into the Chauncey Bottomlands and then the river, John D. Martin's Feed and Poultry building held firm. Martin's feed supply was one of the principal suppliers of feed and live poultry, but all of the grain was destroyed and most of the live poultry was killed, except for a couple of fowl that perched on the roof while the flood surged around them. *From the postcard collection of Arnold L. Sweet.*

Unfortunately, the foundation on which the building was set had washed away, and the building was inundated with the floodwater, which destroyed thousands of dollars of high-quality poultry feed, hay and bedding and rendered any remaining feed "fit [only] to fatten swine." All of the live poultry housed in the building were killed, with the exception of a rooster, a cockerel and a turkey that all survived by perching on the building's roof while the flood swept around them. Thick mud covered the floors and interior walls to the level just below where a locally famous hanging wall clock hung. John Martin reported that, "to spite the flood," the old clock pendulum continued to swing, and the clock continued to work. But with the loss of the store and its inventory, the normal supply of feed for local livestock on the west was diminished to nearly zero.[151] However, much in the same way the predicted west side food famine had been prevented by neighboring communities, by Thursday afternoon, Martin had been able to procure a temporary location in a nearby plumbing store and acquired fresh supplies of corn, oats and hay from grain stores and farms west and north of town to once again sell to west side livestock owners.[152]

PURDUE NEVER CANCELED CLASSES

Meanwhile, at Purdue University, Purdue engineers had managed to keep the coal-fired boilers full of water for the university's steam heat by hand-pumping water from the university's swimming pool. After the pool's water had been drained, water was to be pumped from a large well located next to the Heavilon Hall Mechanical Engineering Building. Despite the Thursday *Lafayette Morning Journal* predicting that the university would be forced to close from a lack of means to heat the classes and laboratories, President Stone reported in the *Purdue Exponent* newspaper and the afternoon edition of Thursday's *Lafayette Daily Courier* that the university never closed during the flood event and that "classes are conducted the same as usual."[153]

Since the creep of floodwater up Main, South and Columbia Streets in Lafayette had halted and was just beginning to recede, news began to shift from businesses that were closing to businesses that were still open and conducting normal business. The Dryfus Theatre had announced the cancellation of its show *The Rose Maid* earlier in the week because the flood-damaged railroads had trapped the acting troupe in Danville, Illinois.[154] But, the Family Theater, which was located at the corner of Sixth and Main Streets in Lafayette, remained open because it was safely two blocks farther east than Fourth Street and, hence, two blocks away from where the flood crept at its peak. The Family Theater, which was remodeled from a Presbyterian chapel in 1906, was a popular stop for vaudeville acts and was financially successful enough to have its own independent "special lighting arrangement" in the event of total electrical power failure similar to what occurred during the flood.[155] With a full bill of acts scheduled to perform at the Family Theater and the newspapers promising the quick return of train service, the theater boldly stated in the *Lafayette Daily Courier* that it "has not closed and has no intention of closing."[156]

Listed in the Thursday *Daily Courier* as "probably the only industrial plant [in Lafayette] not affected by the flood," the Bohrer Brewing Company, located at South Fourth and Alabama Streets in Lafayette, continued to produce brewery products. The plant itself was located on higher ground and was farther from the river than the Thieme and Wagner Brewery across town that had been inundated by the flood. The original owner and builder of the brewery, John H. Newman, and his partner who later succeeded him, George A. Bohrer, built the plant to run independently of local utilities, with its own pump-driven well, a mechanism to generate its own electricity and its own heating plant.[157] The artesian spring, which constituted the source of water for the Bohrer Brewing Company, continued to flow even during the flood, as did the Bohrer Brewing Company's production of beer and spring water.[158]

New Wave of Terror: Wall of Water Coming from Upstream

Although the flood had crested and was falling in Tippecanoe County, there was still concern about the events that were occurring upstream on the Wabash River. At 11:30 a.m. on Thursday, a report came into Lafayette via the Bell Telephone Company line from Chicago and over the Associated Press line from Indianapolis that the Grand Reservoir Dam in Celina, Ohio, had failed, unleashing a tremendous volume of water. The headwaters for the Wabash River are near Fort Recovery, Ohio, about thirty miles across the Indiana-Ohio border and about fifteen miles on a straight line from the Celina Reservoir. A tributary that drains the reservoir dumps into the Wabash River not far from Fort Recovery, and the concern was that the immense volume of water released from the reservoir could elevate the river level at least ten feet all along its downstream path.[159] Once again, the specter of destructive floodwaters appeared just as hope was returning.

The Lafayette authorities wasted little time in mobilizing all police officers to notify all residents on Fourth, Fifth and Sixth Streets north of Cincinnati Street to immediately vacate their homes. All available moving vans and wagons were brought in, and people frantically moved their belongings to other homes, vacant buildings and storage areas to wait out the flood resurgence. It was not until several hours later that a second report arrived, stating that the information about the failure of the Celina Reservoir Dam was an error.[160] The next day, the *Lafayette Daily Courier* reported that the Celina Reservoir had been declared to be safe and that the water level had been lowered, eliminating any immediate risk of dam failure.[161]

Communication Resumes Across the River

On Thursday, efforts had already begun to reestablish communication and commerce across the river, even while the Wabash continued to flow at high flood levels. Although brave souls—or foolish souls, depending on the point of view—had ventured across the railroad bridge earlier in the week

The single operational phone on the west side was located at the Jaques and Southworth Bookstore on State Street, which was a block east from where the Purdue Memorial Union stands today. People lined up for hours to place a thirty-second phone call. *Photograph from the collection of Pete Bill.*

by crawling over the top of the coal cars that were parked on the bridge, by Thursday, deputies were deployed on the west railroad embankment twenty-four hours a day to keep citizens, especially Purdue students keen to see the destruction firsthand, from attempting to cross the railroad bridge. With the Main Street Bridge likewise barricaded and the Brown Street Bridge washed out, there was no easy means by which people could get across the Wabash River in the Lafayette area. Thus, with the water receding, attention began to turn toward identifying a means by which folks could get across the river. At the Monon (railroad) Shops north of town, the Lafayette Engineering Company, the company that had built bridges at Granville, Davis Ferry and Jewettsport, began constructing a ferry boat that would be stationed at the Main Street Bridge to ferry people, wagons and livestock across the river until the bridges could be repaired or replaced.[162]

Telephone communication from the west side to the rest of the world was still limited because, with the exception of the single Bell Telephone Company line, the phone wires carried across the river by the Brown Street and the Main Street Bridges were either completely severed or severely damaged. The single remaining Bell Telephone Company line had Purdue University students and west side citizens lined up at Jaques and Southworth Bookstore at 308–310 State Street for hours to use their phone to call out-of-town relatives.[163] By Thursday afternoon, Frank O. Cuppy, the manager of the Lafayette Telephone Company, had crossed the Main Street Bridge, tracing the telephone cable, and found that the cable was intact where it crossed the bridge and had only been damaged at the Lafayette side of the bridge after the bridge had sagged. The damaged cable was reconnected, reestablishing communication from the west side with the main telephone trunk, thus allowing west side callers to successfully place calls to all points, both local and distant. In addition to the communication wires, an additional electrical line had to be run from the Lafayette Telephone Company to the west side to charge the batteries necessary for the telephone equipment to operate. Had this electrical "charging line" not been strung, the batteries that operated the phone equipment on the west side would have only lasted for a few hours before failing.[164] Although telephone service was now restored to the west side, the large demand to make telephone calls required that all calls be limited to thirty seconds.[165]

Risk of Fatal Conflagration Still High

Although the utility companies had made progress to reestablish service on both sides of the Wabash River, the water shortage was still looming in Lafayette on Thursday, raising continued concern over fire. As of Thursday, the boilers that were needed to drive the water pumps in both the Lafayette and West Lafayette pumphouses still could not be lit, meaning that no water could be pumped to replace the depleted water tank on the west side or refill the Columbian Park Reservoir in Lafayette. By Thursday evening, the pump room at the Lafayette Waterworks still had three and a half feet of standing muddy floodwater, but the engineers were hopeful that the steadily dropping river level would allow the boilers to be started sometime on Friday. However, as of 6:00 p.m. on Thursday, the water level in the Columbian Park Reservoir was only nine feet three inches and was predicted to be exhausted by noon on Friday.[166] Should a fire have erupted in Lafayette or West Lafayette, it was doubtful that there would be enough water to keep it from spreading. With the west side's water tank empty, water with which to fight fires in West Lafayette would only be available from private water cisterns at homes that still had them.[167]

At 2:50 p.m. on Thursday, it appeared that Lafayette's greatest fear might come to pass when an alarm sounded for a fire breaking out at the livery barn on the southeast corner of Fourth and South Streets, an area that was filled with other liveries, the Bramble House hotel, the Lafayette Telephone Company and, only a block north, the large George A. Bohrer Brewing Company. Fires in liveries were especially hazardous because of the presence of hay for bedding and their mostly wooden construction. Citizens were likely surprised—and perhaps alarmed—that, in response to the fire call, the old fire engine steamer, a relic that hadn't been used for years, was seen being pulled to the alarm site by a team of horses supplied by the Winski Junk Company (which was formed in 1907 and is today called the Oscar Winski Company). The fire authorities in the city had moved the old steamer from its storage place on Purdue Street, close to Columbian Park, to the Central Station, which was located downtown on Fourth Street between Brown and Ferry, so as to provide service should a fire break out in downtown Lafayette. Fortunately for all concerned, the alarm turned out to be false—the city must have breathed a sigh of relief.[168] So, the race between the need to light the boilers for the water pumps and the dwindling water supply continued throughout Thursday and into Friday.

Even though the river level was falling, the water was still high, forceful and capable of causing destruction. All houseboats and wharves on the west side of the river had been torn loose and thrown against the railroad bridge over the previous two days. On Thursday morning, around 10:00 a.m., the *Aronzon*, a houseboat owned by Captain W.C. Mitchell, became the last casualty of the boats moored along the west bank of the river when it ripped away from its moorings and smashed into the railroad bridge, turning it instantly into floating wood and debris. The Purdue Club's wharf was finally torn from its rigging on the west bank and sank after floating for a short distance in the turbulent flood. By midday on Thursday, nothing was left standing on the west bank except for a single houseboat that belonged to Mart Barnes.[169] Across the river, on the Lafayette side, the *Lafayette Morning Journal* reported that only two boats remained attached to the east bank of the Wabash. The sternwheeler *Cayuga*, which would play a role in transporting people and goods in the days after the flood, was still lashed by large ropes to sturdy buildings on the east bank, as was the houseboat that was owned by William Randolph. Although both boats were still floating on river water high enough to be level with the brick pavers on Columbia Street, both boats were expected to survive.[170]

Farther north from Lafayette, so-called clubhouses on the Wabash Riverbanks survived the flood, owing to their higher locations. The *Lafayette Daily Courier* reported that the clubhouses near Tecumseh's Trail, located on the high river bluff across River Road from the Indiana Soldiers' Home (now Indiana Veterans' Home), and those clubs located farther north at Birmingham Bluffs (where today's Interstate 65 crosses the Wabash) had managed to survive the flood unscathed. The Riverside Club, a popular club with students and local citizens that was established in 1911 and located on the higher western banks of the Wabash River north of West Lafayette, "stood through all the fury of the waters."[171]

As the cold night fell over the community on Thursday night, the receding Wabash River was relatively quiet as compared to the previous evening, when the intermittent crash of debris against the railroad bridge punctuated the darkness. By 11:00 p.m. on Thursday, the Ydrad Boat Clubhouse near the Main Street Bridge had reported that the water had fallen thirty-three inches and that the floodwater was still dropping at three inches per hour. By Thursday night, it looked like the next day would mark the beginning of the community's recovery process.

Chapter 7

RECOVERY AND HEALING

Friday, March 28, 1913, and Beyond

As another cold March morning dawned over Tippecanoe County, people arose and began the long, slow process of returning to their normal lives. For the previous forty-eight hours, the temperatures had been below freezing, and the weather forecast for Friday, March 28, 1913, did not promise warmer temperatures. The newspapers reported that the cities on both sides of the Wabash River had survived "the worst [flood] in the history of the city."[172] Indeed, the official 32.9 foot crest of the 1913 flood was almost 2 feet higher than the 31.1 foot crest of the 1883 flood that still lingered in the memory of many Tippecanoe County citizens.[173] The *Lafayette Daily Courier* estimated the total loss of property, equipment, personal items and supplies in the Lafayette area to have exceeded $500,000, which, in 2020, would top $12,000,000.[174]

While news from Tippecanoe County was typically crowded off of newspaper pages by more dramatic flood stories from Fort Wayne, Indianapolis and Peru in Indiana and by similar reports from cities in Ohio, occasionally, information about Tippecanoe County reached other states. But, in keeping with the culture of news reporting of the day, this information was not always correct. One New York newspaper reported that two thousand students at Purdue were starving and that the "entire city of Lafayette [had been] wiped off the map." Even in places as close as Illinois, one paper reported that Lafayette "had been swept clean of buildings up to the foot of Oakland Hill."[175] Editors in many newspapers, including the local Tippecanoe County papers, decried the yellow journalism (sensationalizing the news) rampant in some newspapers across the country that had told of greatly exaggerated death tolls, destruction and bizarre flood-related stories.[176]

Back in Tippecanoe County, speculation and proposals were being put forth to the county commissioners on how future destruction could be avoided. It was generally accepted that the sturdy railroad bridge and embankment on the west side had acted as a dam, causing the floodwater to back up and inundate the lowlands between the embankment and the Main Street Levee, destroying the large livestock sales barn, the Esterline Company and many other structures in the lowlands.[177] It was suggested that the New York Central System should cut culverts or make waterways under the embankment to allow floodwater to flow under the earthen dam created by the embankment and prevent future flooding upstream.[178] It was pointed out that the Main Street Levee had also acted as another dam, trapping floodwater that had poured over the adjacent Brown Street Levee into the basin between the levees, flooding the West Lafayette Coal Company's barn and sweeping away buildings and homes. It was suggested that instead of a solid embankment, the Main Street Levee should be replaced with a series of bridges under which floodwater could readily flow.[179] The damage to the Brown Street Levee and the loss of the end of the Brown Street Bridge raised the argument that both the levee and the bridge should be abandoned completely.[180] But all of these plans were for someday in the future; at that moment, attention needed to be directed at the community returning to a more normal life.

Assessing the Damage as the Water Recedes

As the water receded from the west side, the extent of the damage to the Brown Street and Main Street Levees became visible. The Brown Street Levee, which was the less substantially constructed of the two levees, was reduced to a long elevated row of eroded dirt extending from Ellsworth Road (River Road) to the mound of dirt that represented all that what was left of the west abutment of the bridge from where Wangerin and Burkhouse had been rescued by Dr. Whitesell.

The Main Street Levee had been more substantially constructed than the Brown Street Levee. The Main Street Levee had a concrete base that was

After the flood, this furrowed row of dirt was all that remained of the Brown Street Levee and the road that ran to the Brown Street Bridge. The flood current flowed from left to right, cascading over the levee and washing away the soil. *From the postcard collection of Arnold L. Sweet.*

The Brown Street Levee, looking from the river toward the Coal Company barn and Chauncey Hill. By the time this photograph was taken, a rough grading had created a crude dirt road along the levee. The large dirt mound to the right was all that remained of the long, elevated bridge approach on which Wangerin and Burkhouse stood after the Brown Street Bridge collapsed. *From the postcard collection of Arnold L. Sweet.*

covered by a thick layer of asphalt, allowing the Main Street Levee to carry both wagon and pedestrian traffic and the rail line for the Fort Wayne and Northern Indiana Traction Company electric trolley cars. Poured-concrete sidewalks and power poles carrying electrical and telephone lines from Lafayette flanked the Main Street Levee, and brick and wooden buildings lined the length of the levee all the way to the river. As such, the Main Street Levee was thought to present a "grand entrance way," welcoming those who crossed the Main Street Bridge to the growing west side.

During the early stages of the flood, the water filling the lowland basins to the north of Brown and Main Streets was funneled through the lowest part of the levee in front of the Morgan and Torrenga garage at the foot of State Street (Chauncey) Hill, concentrating the force of the floodwater that tore away the pavement, gouged out the softened soil beneath it and formed a channel that was at least ten feet deep. This channel extended to the Main Street Levee, where the force of the water undermined the roadway, allowing the railroad ties and steel streetcar rails to sink into the resulting hole. The force of the water cascading over the levee and dropping into the Chauncey Bottomlands swept away the remaining levee asphalt, the sidewalks and the toppled powerlines. The force of the water falling into the basin swept away dirt foundations from around buildings along

The force of the floodwater that cascaded over the Main Street Levee and into the Chauncey Bottomlands was evidenced by the depth of the craters around the foundation of this precariously teetering building. *From the postcard collection of Arnold L. Sweet.*

The Main Street Levee, looking up State Street Hill (Chauncey Hill). The force of the floodwater that flowed over the levee eroded the soil away from both sides of the traction line tracks, creating a deep trench on the right and ripping away paved roadways and sidewalks on the left. *From the postcard collection of Arnold L. Sweet.*

the Main Street Levee, tipping or toppling the foundations and destroying the buildings on which they rested. The only buildings still left on the south side of the Main Street Levee were the remnants of the Martin Produce Store, the Jamison Garage and another small building that was perched precariously on a ten-foot-high, narrow stone foundation, devoid of any surrounding soil. The only evidence remaining of the veterinary infirmary from where Dr. Whitesell had launched his boat to rescue the men stranded after the Brown Street Bridge collapse was the concrete approach to where it had once stood. The degree of levee desolation demonstrated, once again, the destructive force of the water.[181]

UTILITIES BEGIN TO RECOVER

On the morning of Friday, March 28, 1913, the *Lafayette Morning Journal* reported that the river was still falling at the rate of three to four inches per hour. By late Friday morning, the relatively rapid recession of the flood's edge allowed the engineers at the gas and electrical utility plants to complete their damage assessments and begin the process of restarting boilers and other equipment that were needed for the delivery of essential utilities. By 4:00 p.m. on Friday, William Wallace, the superintendent of the Indiana Lighting Gas Company, succeeded in starting one of the two gas-generating machines. Even though the second gas engine was predicted to begin running at midnight, illuminating gas would not be available to consumers until both of the large gas storage tanks were filled—a process that would take at least another twelve hours.[182] The Saturday *Lafayette Daily Courier* reported that gas would be pumped into the city's gas mains (pipelines) at 3:00 p.m. on Saturday afternoon. By Saturday evening, food was again being cooked with gas, and hot meals were being enjoyed for the first time since the flood had begun.[183]

The Merchants Electrical Light Association, which also served as Lafayette's city heating plant, was able to get its boilers online again to offer hot water by midday Saturday, March 29, but the two big direct-current generators that supplied electricity were extensively damaged by water. The separate generators that supplied street lighting escaped damage because they were located in a higher area within the building. By Saturday afternoon, the association had reported that some of the lighting machinery would be running by 6:00 p.m. on Saturday evening and that people who had Merchants Electrical Light Association lights could have illumination back by Saturday night.[184]

By Sunday afternoon, the Merchants Electrical Light Association engineers had managed to get all of the equipment functioning, and after a few faltering tries, the streetlights came on and stayed on at 6:30 p.m. on Sunday. The restoration of the streetlights represented the final restoration of electrical utilities.[185]

Even though the Lafayette Waterworks was still inundated with muddy water as of Thursday evening—and thus unable to reignite its boilers to begin pumping water—the smaller West Lafayette Pumphouse recorded only three inches of water on the pumphouse floor at 10:00 p.m. Thursday. Shortly thereafter, the boilers needed to generate steam to drive the water pumps were reignited and began heating the boiler water. By Friday morning, the steam boilers were driving the west side's water pumps, and the water tank at the top of Grant and Salisbury Streets began to fill with much-needed clean, fresh and readily available water.[186] However, even as the west side pumps began working again, it was found that the floodwater had washed through the walls of the pumphouse and had possibly weakened a main partition that supported the entire pumphouse, creating fear that the structure would collapse. Pumping stopped for several hours, but by Saturday morning, the pumphouse walls were declared sound enough to support the building, and water operations for West Lafayette resumed.[187]

Meanwhile in Lafayette, the water supply from the Columbian Park Reservoir was exhausted by Friday morning.[188] When chief engineer Colonel Thomas McDowell arrived at the Canal Street Lafayette Pumping Station at 5:00 a.m. on Friday, five inches of floodwater still covered the floor of the engine room. But because the floodwater was dropping so quickly, by mid-morning on Friday, the floodwater was gone. However, everything in the pump house was covered by two inches of mud. The water company crews quickly cleared the mud, and by 11:00 a.m. on Friday morning, one of the large pumps began forcing water into the huge Lafayette water mains. By 1:00 p.m. on Friday, the water had reached the Oak Hill neighborhood on top of the east escarpment across the street from the Columbian Park Reservoir. By 5:00 p.m. on Friday evening, the reservoir held four feet of water and was continuing to fill.[189] Even though the pumps were operating, they were not running at their full capacity and would require at least another twenty-four hours before the Columbian Park Reservoir would be filled with enough water to provide ample fire protection.[190] Thus, the Lafayette citizenry were advised to continue being vigilant with the use of any open flames, as any outbreak of fire might not be extinguished with the diminished supply of water available.[191]

Throughout Saturday, the reservoir at Columbian Park continued to slowly fill, and by Saturday evening, limited water service had been restored to most of Lafayette. Even as water service was improving, the water company advised that all water used for drinking, regardless of whether it came from personal wells or the city's own water mains, should be boiled to avoid an outbreak of typhoid and diarrheal diseases like cholera.[192] At the same time that the water company issued what we would today call a "boil order," the Lafayette city health department announced that it would be taking charge of disinfecting all the flooded houses and buildings that contained layers of muddy Wabash River sludge. By order of the city, all dwellings or buildings would have to be disinfected and put into "proper sanitary condition" before residents could be allowed to return.[193]

The Trains Attempt to Run Again

It is difficult to conceptualize from today's perspective how dependent the 1913 Tippecanoe County community was on an effective rail system for their normal daily life. Thus, it was huge news when the Monon; Lake Erie and Western; Wabash; and Big Four Railroads all announced, on the morning of Friday, March 28, that some degree of limited train traffic would begin running to, from and through Lafayette.[194] Wallace Marshall of the Lafayette Engineering Company examined the railroad bridge and found that the first span had been forced out of alignment by slightly over an inch, but the pier itself (on which the span rested) seemed solid and did not appear to be undermined as the Main Street Bridge pier had been. It would come to pass that superficial appearances of the railroad bridge's piers would be deceiving.

On Friday morning, a coal train without passengers was sent slowly over the railroad bridge to test for stability. Having passed that test successfully, at 9:30 a.m. Friday, March 28, a southbound Lake Erie and Western (LE&W) train from Kankakee, Illinois, with over one hundred passengers crossed the bridge at two miles per hour. With the opening of this critical railroad bridge, the LE&W and the Big Four Rail Lines could resume rail traffic between Chicago and Indianapolis. In addition to the regular freight and passenger rail traffic, the LE&W Railroad would begin running shuttle trains across the bridge at irregular intervals to transport people between Lafayette and West Lafayette. Although the shuttle got off to a slow start on Friday, as word spread, crowds waiting for the shuttle grew, and by Saturday, the LE&W Railroad had established a regular hourly shuttle that also included the use of some railcars to accommodate buggies and horses.[195]

The regular trains of the Big Four and Lake Erie Lines, which both used the railroad bridge, were required to drive so slowly across the embankment and bridge that people would often jump onto the lumbering trains and ride across the river, using them as unintentional shuttles.[196] In spite of the relief the regular the LE&W shuttle provided, residents soon became frustrated, as large crowds and long lines of businessmen and consumers waited to get to the other side of the river. The problem with the great demand was quickly noticed by the local press, and the newspapers admonished Purdue students and residents without important business across the river to find other means by which to cross the river.[197]

Although regular rail service through Lafayette had been reestablished by Saturday afternoon for the Big Four and the LE&W railroads, the Monon System was still unable to provide service through Lafayette because the Monon track north of Lafayette was still washed out. However, regular Monon service between Battleground, which was located on the other side of the Monon track washout, and Chicago had already resumed, and with its southern Indiana

Crowds wait on the west side's railroad embankment and bridge over Ellsworth Road for space on the Lake Erie & Western shuttle train that ran hourly across the Wabash River. The shuttle was a relatively inefficient means of conveying hundreds of citizens across the Wabash River each day, so it was quickly supplemented by ferry barge traffic. *From the postcard collection of Arnold L. Sweet.*

rail segments still intact, the Monon was able to use its railway network to bypass Lafayette and reestablish rail traffic between Chicago and the cities on the Ohio River. The fourth major steam rail line, the Wabash Railroad, had no problem re-establishing service from Peru, Indiana, through Lafayette and west as far as Danville, Illinois, and St. Louis, but its eastern track segment ended at Peru, where the flood damage was more extensive than it had been in Tippecanoe County. Only passengers transporting essential freight could travel east from Lafayette to Peru on the Wabash Railroad because there were no accommodations available in Peru for visitors or curiosity seekers.[198]

As the major rail lines worked to reconnect Tippecanoe County to the rest of the nation, the electric traction companies (electric rail, the interurban) so essential for the daily transportation of people between cities within Indiana, were likewise recovering. The Terre Haute, Indianapolis and Eastern Traction company (THI&E), one of the two traction lines servicing Lafayette, began regularly running cars again between Lafayette, Lebanon and Crawfordsville on Friday, March 29. The THI&E had the advantage of servicing southern routes from Tippecanoe County, which meant their lines did not have to cross the Wabash River or its major tributaries. Unfortunately, the Fort Wayne and Northern Indiana Traction Company, which ran service between Lafayette and Fort Wayne in the eastern part of the state, had many of its bridges destroyed by the flood, including the one that spanned Wildcat Creek in Tippecanoe County. The Fort Wayne Traction Company estimated it would be as long as two weeks before this link between Lafayette and all points north and east to Fort Wayne could be re-established.[199] Ironically, this news hit the heroes of the Fort Wayne and Northern Indiana's powerhouse hard, as they had fought to maintain a supply of electrical power to the city after the larger Merchants Electric Light Association Company plant had been inundated and shut down by the flood. In spite of having no railcars running that would need its electricity, the Fort Wayne and Northern Powerhouse continued to produce electricity that was distributed to the rest of the electrical grid of the city.

OTHER SIGNS OF NORMAL LIFE BEGIN TO RETURN

On Saturday, March 29, the school superintendent announced that the public schools, which had been closed since Wednesday due to the limited drinking water supply, would reopen on Monday, March 31, providing the community with another sign of a rapid return to normalcy.[200]

Amid of the throes of the flood, the cessation of mail delivery service to Tippecanoe County citizens was scarcely noticed. However, the county's main post office, located at Fourth and Ferry Streets in downtown Lafayette, was within the flood zone, and Postmaster Haywood and his employees were fighting to keep the bags of mail safe from the rising water. To add to the challenge, mail continued to arrive on the few trains that were able to run into Lafayette from the south and the west. By Saturday, March 29, the *Lafayette Daily Courier* had reported that the post office was swamped with a huge number of mail bags stacked on tables above the floodwater in the building and that mail delivery would begin again that day. Postmaster Haywood and his assistant William E. Work put every postal employee to work delivering the mail. At the same time that Haywood was mobilizing his employees to tackle the backlog of mail sitting in the Lafayette post office, the Monon Railroad notified the post office that it had delivered twenty-two pouches of first-class mail and many more sacks of second-class mail to Battleground that were intended for delivery to Lafayette. Because the washed-out Monon tracks north of the town prevented the railroad from completing the delivery to Lafayette, three postal employees loaded up an automobile with eight hundred pounds of outgoing mail from the Lafayette Post Office and drove the twenty-two minutes to Battleground to load their

The Lafayette Post Office building at Fourth and Ferry Streets (the same location where the modern post office stands today). The floodwater rose high enough to cover these streets and pour into the lower level of the post office, threatening the mail stored in the basement. *From the postcard collection of Arnold L. Sweet.*

mail on an outgoing, northbound Monon train and retrieve the incoming mail bags destined for Lafayette.[201]

Because the newspapers continued to warn their readers to boil all water to avoid cholera and other flood-related illnesses, the local bottling companies found a new market for the water they used in their distilling process. The Bohrer Bottling Works advertised in the April 2 edition of the *Lafayette Daily Courier* that the noted Purdue University sanitary science bacteriologist Severence Burrage, BS, PhD, had endorsed its product with the words, "Your distilled water indicates an excellent degree of purity. I do not hesitate to recommend your distilled water most highly."[202] The bottles of such water commanded a premium price at $1.50 per dozen bottles, which would be equivalent to $38.85 in 2020. However, the diligent purchaser could get a rebate of $0.50 ($12.95 in 2020) for returning all twelve empty bottles. It can be presumed that such disease-fueled sales of bottled drinking water were short-lived when articles began to appear the next day in the local newspapers, citing the results of water analyses performed by Purdue University that affirmed the city water was "free from infection and boiling [was] not necessary." [203] Even with such testimony, there was still skepticism about the purity of the local water supply. The average citizen did not

The interior of the Lafayette Post Office building. The postal workers moved all of the mail bags from the basement to the main floor, occupying most of the tabletop and floor space. On Sunday, March 30, the post office announced in the *Lafayette Morning Journal*, "Please come and get your mail." *Photograph courtesy of Tippecanoe County Historical Association.*

possess a good understanding of the inherent safety of the deep aquifers from which Lafayette obtained its water and instead assumed the water in their taps came directly from the muddy, debris-filled Wabash River or from shallow wells typical of farms and homes. This misconception was fueled by the newspapers that recommended the local water supply be "closely scrutinized" weekly until "all water which has been coursing through stable yards, and cesspools, and in contact with human excreta, is accounted for." They continued, "The water is alright now, but there is no telling when water, which was once floodwater, will find its way underground and appear in our water supply."[204]

Oscar Winski and Company (the Winski Junk Company that provided horses to pull the old fire apparatus through downtown during a fire false alarm) took advantage of the surplus of flood-damaged machinery and equipment to advertise that it would "pay you a good price" for "all kinds of damaged merchandise and machinery."[205] Today, the Oscar Winski Company, which was founded in 1907, still does business in Tippecanoe County as a metal scrap recycler and redistributor.

THE GRIM TASKS

One of the grimmer aspects of the recovery process was the mobilization of families and neighbors to begin the task of trying to find the bodies of those who had been swept away by the floodwaters. On the morning of Friday, March 28, the people of Mulberry, Indiana, turned out under clear but cold skies to search for the bodies of Ray and Roscoe Rothenberger, who had been swept away in Wildcat Creek after their boat overturned five days earlier. The accident occurred on the southern fork of Wildcat Creek, near the Wyandotte Bridge, which was located three and a half miles due west of Mulberry next to the now-vanished village of Wyandot (the Wyandot Post Office existed from 1849 to 1872). The boat—and presumably the bodies—would have been carried northward to where Wildcat Creek's south fork joined the middle fork before eventually flowing into the Wabash River. The search party began its search at the Wyandotte Bridge (the *Lafayette Morning Journal* spelled Wyandot "Wyandotte," which is the more common spelling used today) and followed the winding banks six miles northward to where the middle fork joined the southern fork north of what is today State Road 26, near Monitor. Failing to find anything, the search party continued following the fork to the main Wildcat Creek, another three miles northwestward to near what is today Eisenhower Road.[206] The *Lafayette Daily Courier* reported that, as of Thursday, April 3, the efforts to recover the bodies had failed.[207] However, on April 8, the body of Ray Rothenberger was found in the creek bottom near where his boat had overturned by the Wyandotte Bridge.[208] On April 27, two hundred people from Mulberry and the surrounding areas, including church congregations that normally would have been in Sunday morning church services, performed one final search of Wildcat Creek from Wyandotte Bridge to the town of Dayton for the body of Roscoe Rothenberger.[209] Unfortunately, the body of Roscoe Rothenberger was never found.

F.P. Woolery, the father of Leland Woolery, the Purdue student who had died in the failed attempt to rescue Paul Wangerin and Charles Burkhouse from the west embankment of the collapsed Brown Street Bridge, arrived in West Lafayette on the afternoon of Friday, March 28, to help with the efforts to find the body of his son.[210] Unfortunately, at the time of his arrival, the high floodwaters hampered access to many areas of the riverbanks. It was not until 9:45 a.m. on Saturday, April 5, that Leland Woolery's body was discovered entangled in fence wire and debris in front of the Detention Hospital just south of the railroad bridge.[211] Because the railroad bridge

The Detention Hospital south of the railroad bridge. L.P. Woolery's body was found on April 5, 1913, in the debris that is marked by the "X" on the left side of the photograph. The county coroner and L.P. Woolery's uncle Dr. Homer Woolery supervised the body's removal and transported it by boat back to the Main Street Levee. L.P. Woolery's pocket watch was found in his vest and had stopped at 2:15 p.m., the time of the accident. *From the postcard collection of Arnold L. Sweet.*

embankments on either side of the river had created a narrows through which the full current of the flood was forced to flow, a large whirlpool had formed in the wider area just downstream of the bridge in front of the Detention Hospital. Into this whirlpool, large amounts of floating debris from the destruction of the buildings on the bottomlands between the Main Street Levee and the railroad embankment had accumulated. The debris hid Woolery's body until the water receded enough for the body to be found by E. Stockton and F. Houlihan, two employees of the transfer and livery company owned by the Stockton brothers, who were searching for livery equipment that had been lost after the company barn and its equipment were swept into the main current of the river.[212] Purdue University memorialized Woolery on Memorial Day, May 29, 1913, during exercises held in Fowler Hall, and a tablet was presented that would be displayed in the Memorial Gymnasium erected in 1908 to honor the lives of those who were lost in the 1903 train wreck.[213] Today, the building still stands on Purdue's campus as Felix Haas Hall.

FERRIES ACROSS THE WABASH

For several days after the flood, the New York Central System Railroad Bridge was the only bridge still functioning that connected Lafayette and West Lafayette. The LE&W Railroad continued to run a shuttle back and forth across the bridge, but it became rapidly apparent by the long lines of people waiting to take the shuttle across the river that alternatives for getting across the river were needed. Shortly after the Wabash River level began falling, the Lafayette Engineering Company began constructing a ferry boat for transporting people between First Street on the Lafayette bank to the Main Street Levee on the west side.[214] Poles were set into the ground on either bank, and cables were strung across the river to allow the ferry to be manually pulled by hand from one side to the other. The final caulking of the seams of the ferry barge and the application of oakum tar were completed on Tuesday, April 1, with the intent to launch the ferry on Wednesday, April 2.[215] Even though the Lafayette Engineering ferry barge was ready, the ferry service would not be approved to transport people until the cables that would guide the ferry barge were tested. And testing of the guide cables could not occur until the water level fell sufficiently enough that the current would not push on the ferry barge with such force that the guide cable would snap. Since they had to wait for the river level to fall, the prediction for the beginning of operations of the ferry service was pushed back until Monday, April 7.[216]

Unfortunately, at 1:30 p.m. on April 2, the Lake Erie and Western Railroad authorities suddenly stopped all rail traffic across the bridge.[217] A closer inspection of the railroad bridge revealed that one of the stone bridge piers had sunk four inches, and the spans resting on the pier had pulled the track rails two and a half inches out of line, rendering the bridge unsafe for rail passage. Passengers aboard Lake Erie and Western or Big Four trains had to disembark on one side of the river, hike down the muddy embankment, wait in line for a ferry or other boat to take them to the other side, then board another train to continue their journey.[218]

The cessation of the rail shuttle ratcheted up the need for the ferry service across the river. Private owners of watercraft had independently begun filling this need even before the Lafayette Engineering Company ferry barge had been completed. Captain Peter A. Kennedy, the owner of the power sternwheeler *Cayuga*, was the first to announce that his ferry service between the Columbia Street Wharf on the Lafayette side to the Main Street Levee would begin Friday, March 28. The *Cayuga*'s powerful twelve-horsepower gasoline engine could propel it and up to fifty passengers across the Wabash

The ferry barges, including the Lafayette Engineering Company Barge, shown here, were pulled across the river along cables that were strung between poles on the opposite banks. With all bridges closed, the slow barges were the only means by which individuals could cross the river, resulting in large crowds on both banks waiting to cross. *From the postcard collection of Arnold L. Sweet.*

River in two to three minutes for the fee of five cents per person, which, as Captain Kennedy claimed, was only enough to cover the cost of the gasoline.[219] In addition to transporting passengers, Captain Kennedy and the *Cayuga* were instrumental in helping to stretch the cables across the river that would guide and pull the nonmotorized Lafayette Engineering Company ferry barge across the river.[220]

Other smaller motorboat owners began seizing on the opportunity to cash in on the new demand for ferry service, charging anywhere from no fee (passengers would pay what they wanted or nothing at all) to twenty-five cents, which was considered "scandalously high" for a one-way ride. Some of the southside Lafayette neighborhood O'Connor boys were considered excellent "rivermen," and rising to the occasion, they rigged up a small passenger and freight barge, connected it to a small motor skiff and powered it across the river loaded with ten to twelve passengers and all manner of merchandise, fruit, bakery products and laundry.[221]

Challenges to safe ferry barge transport became apparent early on in the days of the ferries due to rising and falling river levels and the impact of storms, waves, wind or fast currents. The unpowered cabled ferries would turn sideways in strong currents or winds, and the lateral forces would pull

The sternwheeler *Cayuga*, captained by Peter A. Kennedy, was one of the few large riverboats moored on the Wabash River to survive the flood. Its twelve-horsepower gasoline engine was capable of carrying up to fifty passengers between the Columbia Street Wharf and the west bank, even if weather or river conditions became too rough for the cable-drawn ferries to safely operate. *From the postcard collection of Arnold L. Sweet.*

People, wagons and freight all crowded onto the ferry barges. Owners of small powerboats and rowboats made good money transporting small groups of people across the river, as they were far quicker and ran more frequently than the ferry barges. *From the postcard collection of Arnold L. Sweet.*

The O'Connor boys, the experienced rivermen from Lafayette's south side, figured out a way to hook up their powerboat and drive a barge across the river more quickly than the cable-pulled barges. Because their services were in such high demand, motorized craft pilots could charge as much as twenty-five cents per passenger. *Photograph courtesy of Tippecanoe County Historical Association.*

the cable sideways dangerously hard. On Monday, April 7, soon after the ferry barge service had begun, a ferry with one hundred men, women and children broke loose from the cable and threatened to dash its occupants against the railroad bridge pier or sweep them downstream. Fortunately, the O'Connor boys, with their powered skiff and other motorboats, were able to keep the runaway ferry barge in the channel between the railroad bridge piers. As the barge passed under the railroad bridge, men up on the tracks threw ropes to the barge, which were quickly tied to the barge, "capturing" it just past the railroad bridge. The powerboats took the frightened women and children from the barge and safely transported them to the western shore. Ladders were lowered from the bridge to the ferry, and dozens of men climbed them to safety. The near disaster made obvious that a more permanent solution would be needed to safely and efficiently transport people and freight across the river.

Even with the risks, the makeshift ferry system was in high demand, and ferry transports ran from 5:00 a.m. until midnight every day, with some smaller craft continuing to operate into the dark hours of the early morning. The *Cayuga* alone reported transporting two thousand passengers in one day.[222] Even though high water and fast currents had been the initial threats to the cabled ferries and other watercraft, the rapidly dropping river level also exposed another different type of threat. As the river level returned to pre-flood levels, a sandbar emerged forty feet from the west bank and in the direct cable path of the main ferry. As the river level continued to fall, the sand bar eventually prevented the ferry from being able to float across the river, completely halting operations for several days. A 0.68-inch rainfall raised the river level high enough to allow the ferry to operate again.[223]

In spite of the ferry system and numerous small craft used to transport people across the river, the transportation was still very inefficient, resulting in long lines waiting to cross. Attention in the community turned again to the idea of building some form of a bridge—even a temporary bridge—to relieve the daily demand by citizens to reach the other bank. One such stopgap measure, reported by the *Indianapolis Star*, involved the Tippecanoe County Commissioners petitioning Senator Kern for the necessary materials and expertise from the U.S. War Department to

Occasionally, the cable used to draw the barge across the river would snap, and the ferry would begin to float downstream with the current. This photograph shows a very crowded "runaway" ferry that floated downstream, barely missing the bridge piers before finally being corralled by powerboaters and ropes that were thrown from the railroad bridge. *From the postcard collection of Arnold L. Sweet.*

construct a pontoon bridge of the type used by the military to convey troops and vehicles across rivers.[224] The War Department responded that the materials for such a bridge were held in reserve for emergency military use and could not be released to Tippecanoe County. As a concession, the War Department directed Captain John Kingman of the U.S. Army Corps of Engineers to visit Lafayette and instruct local engineers on how to construct such a bridge from their own materials. However, once Captain Kingman evaluated the situation in Lafayette, he pronounced the idea of pontoon bridge "insufficient and useless." The degree of the rise and fall of the Wabash River would result in the bridge being torn loose from its shore anchors and being washed away.[225] Thus, the pontoon bridge, along with an idea to build a pedestrian suspension bridge, was just one of several ideas or proposals put forth that never materialized.

The community's frustration with the ferry system also began to grow, just as it had with the rail shuttle system. Mishaps and mechanical failures resulted in additional delays and only added to the frustration of the citizens wanting to get across the river and the owners of the businesses they would frequent. The original cable for the large ferry barge snapped, shutting the ferry down for two days before a new, thicker steel braided cable could be found and restrung across the river. The trusty *Cayuga* was put out of commission for an entire day when the drive chain on the gasoline engine wore out, stalling the *Cayuga* in the middle of the river. High winds and rapid currents frequently took the large ferry barge out of service, and even in good weather, the trip could take at least ten minutes to complete.

Competition between people and wagons for the available space on the *Cayuga* and larger ferry barges often resulted in horse-drawn wagons lining up on Main Street all the way back to Third Street and created delays of more than two hours or more to board. The newspapers had multiple reports of horses becoming agitated or spooked while standing in line, charging off with their wagon load and careening into other wagons, buildings and people. West siders who worked in Lafayette were often delayed in getting to work, and if rumors spread that river conditions were threatening to shut down the ferries, offices in Lafayette would empty of all west side residents who were unwilling to be stranded on the wrong side of the river without a way to get back home. One evening, frustration boiled over into mob rule when two hundred west side residents waiting to board a ferry were told by the ferry master that the wagons that had been waiting to cross would be transported before them and that the crowd would have to wait their turn. Apparently, many in the crowd were intending to attend the Harlequin Club show at the Dryfus Theatre, and as they were not willing to miss the curtain call, they rushed onto the ferry, pushed aside the ferry master and cut the rope that secured the barge to the west bank. The men aboard the ferry, dressed in their fine theater attire, pulled the ferry barge to the other side. After the crowd disembarked on the east side, a smaller group of men stayed on the ferry and pulled it back to the west side, where it was turned back over to the astonished ferrymen. Although the sheriff was called, no arrests were made.[226] However, the incident dramatized the level of frustration citizens experienced with the ferry system.

Downtown Lafayette merchants reported local trade conditions were greatly depressed by the poor traffic connections with West Lafayette and all other points west and north of the city. Because of the imposed ferry restrictions that prevented the transport of uncaged or unharnessed livestock, west side farmers were cut off from moving livestock to the stockyards in Lafayette, and farm produce supply into the city was reduced to a trickle.[227] In an effort to better regulate the ferries for the safety of passengers, on April 7, the county commissioners implemented rules that prohibited livestock or poultry from being transported unless they were securely tied or placed in cages. The new rules also limited the amount of merchandise that could be transported. This did little to alleviate the merchants' and citizens' concerns and reinforced the idea that the only solution would be reopening a bridge.

THE RAILROAD BRIDGE IS THE FIRST TO REOPEN

Because, at first, the New York Central System Railroad Bridge seemed to be the least-damaged of the three main bridges in Lafayette, high hopes had existed for it to reopen quickly. However, within a short period of time after work began to repair the malalignment of the rails noticed earlier in the month, it became obvious that the bridge was more heavily damaged than it appeared from above the surface of the water. The first hint came from a steam-operated pile driver machine positioned against the eastern pier when it began driving the first sixty-foot-long wooden piling (thick poles, like telephone poles) next to the stone pier to give it support. As the long pile was placed on the river bottom for driving, it was discovered that the river bottom around the railroad bridge pier, much like the pier on the Main Street Bridge, had also been scoured by the floodwater, creating a cavity that was at least ten feet deeper than the rest of the riverbed. The longer distance between the bridge decking and the river bottom meant that longer, seventy-foot pilings had to be brought in from Chicago, further delaying the repair work. Additional soundings (done by lowering metal weights on the end of ropes to determine the river bottom contours) revealed that not one, but four of the six railroad bridge piers had been undermined in a similar manner. This meant that instead of reinforcing one pier with wooden pilings, the huge pilings would have to be driven next to four of the six bridge piers.[228]

After it became clear that more damage had been done to the railroad bridge piers than could be assessed from the surface or by the crude method of making soundings, the commissioners and the county engineer consultants mandated a more accurate estimation of the damage to be conducted. Fortunately, the use of the diving suit in 1913 made such work possible. The Lake Erie and Western Railroad enlisted the services of David Hanson, one of the most famous divers in the United States, to visually inspect the piers and assess the situation firsthand. Hanson arrived from Chicago on April 17, and with the help of his assistant, who manually pumped air down into the dive suit, he got to work. Within two days, he had done his assessment and had already placed some sway bracing (crossed metal bands to reduce sideways movement) around the weakened pier to help stabilize it. Hanson would perform additional repairs to reinforce the piers over the next several weeks.[229] In the meantime, with the weakened pier strengthened by Hanson's work and newly constructed false work (wooden scaffolding or other temporary bracings for structural support), the railroad bridge was judged to be strong enough for trains to begin running across it for the first time in over two weeks.[230]

The next step in permanently stabilizing the bridge piers required driving the seventy-foot wooden pilings next to the pier bases and then building coffer dams around the base of the old stone piers to divert the river away from the piers so the piers could be repaired and reinforced with concrete. Several days into the repairs, a huge stone from one of the piers came loose and dropped into the river, taking out the reinforcing pilings on one side and raising alarms about the support of the decking and track resting on that pier. The damage to the pilings occurred only ten minutes before a Big Four passenger train was scheduled to cross the bridge, sending workers scrambling up the tracks to flag down the approaching train before it started to cross the weakened tracks. Fortunately, the damage to the pilings had compromised only the support of the northern set of the two tracks on the bridge, so rail traffic was diverted to the southern tracks, allowing trains to cross safely over the river.

Finally, on August 19, 1913, five months after the bridge had been damaged and most of the extensive repairs to the piers had been completed, trains were allowed to run over both sets of tracks, although still at a slower speed than normal. Work continued for several weeks after the opening, amassing a final cost of over $50,000, roughly equivalent to $1.3 million in today's currency. Today, much of the original stonework of the piers (reinforced with concrete) is still apparent to anyone crossing the river on the nearby Governor Harry G. Leslie vehicle bridge that connects State Street on the west side to South Street on the east. Unlike the original double-tracked bridge in 1913, the old piers now support only a single track, owing to the removal of the second track during the extensive Lafayette railroad relocation project in the mid-1990s. Today, the sturdy, darkened stones still serve as a testament to the engineering that went into the original construction of the bridge and the effectiveness of the extensive repair work done after the 1913 flood.

The Fate of the Brown Street Bridge

Although the railroad bridge repair had been the initial focus for reestablishing effective transportation across the river, it did not directly address the problems with the transportation of most people, vehicles, livestock and merchandise posed by the inadequacy of the ferry system. In response, county commissioners turned their attention to the Brown Street Bridge repair, awarding Wallace Marshall's Lafayette Engineering Company a contract to quickly build a temporary wooden span to connect the remainder of the still-standing Brown Street Bridge to the west bank. The work was delayed because a recent rain had raised the river level three feet, and workers had to wait until the water level dropped sufficiently to be able to use the barge-mounted steam pile driver to place the wooden pilings used to support the decking of the temporary wooden bridge. On April 15, work commenced, and by Saturday, April 26, eleven rows of pilings had been driven into the Wabash's riverbed and the wooden decking put into place. On that Saturday, the first wagons and vehicles rumbled across the bridge.[231] Even though the wooden bridge connected Brown Street in Lafayette to the Brown Street Levee on the west side, the west side's Brown Street Levee was still in poor shape, having only been roughly graded to create a somewhat level path along the top of the eroded dirt embankment. Thus, while vehicular traffic could get across

A pile driver barge places pilings to support a temporary wooden span for the Brown Street Bridge. The twisted steel of the two collapsed bridge spans can be seen in the river in the foreground. *From the postcard collection of Arnold L. Sweet.*

the river, there was still a considerable challenge to reach Ellsworth Road and the bottom of the State Street hill, especially during the rainy spring weather that turned the dirt levee into mud.

It wasn't until July 1913 that the county commissioners put out bids for a steel replacement of the temporary wooden span on the Brown Street Bridge. Further grading and leveling of the Brown Street Levee would also be done, eventually using gravel topped with oil to create a rudimentary roadbed for the summer and fall. But the plans for the levee repair did not include raising the levee to provide better protection for the lower basin between the Main Street and Brown Street Levees from a rising river. On July 9, the Lafayette Engineering Company was awarded the contract to rebuild the Brown Street Bridge stone pier that had collapsed during the flood and build a replacement steel span in a style that matched the ironwork used with the original 1903 bridge construction.[232]

Work began almost immediately on the pier and steel span and was targeted to be completed in November 1913. The Brown Street Bridge would remain open to vehicular traffic over the wooden span until the steel span was ready to be put into place.[233] On October 20, 1913, the Brown Street Bridge was closed so the steel span could be installed. During this time, the old Main Street Bridge, which had been sufficiently repaired to temporarily allow vehicular traffic, was opened to traffic, except for heavy trucks, wagons and vehicles weighing over 4,500 pounds. The officers guarding the Main Street Bridge would then direct wagon teams and vehicles across the bridge at a speed no faster than a slow walk. The city threatened to close the Main Street Bridge again should the rules and speed limit not be strictly followed.[234] By November 21, 1913, the Brown Street Bridge's new steel spans were in place, the Brown Street Levee had been widened and improved with 240 loads of gravel and the community announced that a "new" route had been opened for commerce to come to Lafayette.[235]

The Brown Street Bridge weathered many subsequent floods and ice jams. However, concerns about a second collapse of the Brown Street Bridge resurfaced in 1958 when the high river water was "swirling menacingly around the west abutment of the bridge."[236] Although the bridge was closed temporarily, it reopened soon after the 1958 flood. But in 1973, a county highway supervisor noticed a one-and-a-half-inch drop in the pavement, leading to the subsequent discovery of a twelve-foot crack in the same pier that was constructed to repair the bridge in 1913. The bridge was immediately closed to all traffic.[237] Bridge pier repair began in the summer of 1973, but soon, more cracks were discovered in other piers.

Work delays dragged out the refurbishment of the Brown Street Bridge for a year, into the summer of 1974. Then, on the week of July 4, 1974, almost a year to the date that the first crack had been found, a supporting stone pier was discovered to have dropped an inch in one day and moved two inches laterally. The next day, the north face of the stone pier pivoted slightly and dropped almost a foot, prompting an emergency removal of all the workers on the bridge and the cordoning off the bridge from any boat traffic underneath.[238] In spite of the $150,000 already invested in the repair of the bridge from the summer of 1973 to the summer of 1974, the superstructure of the bridge and the continuing problems with the piers forced the county commissioners to condemn the bridge and order its demolition. In October 1974, the Brown Street Bridge, including the original spans and piers that had survived the 1913 flood, was permanently removed.[239] Today, the western stone abutment of the bridge at the terminus of Brown Street in West Lafayette and a plaque are all that remain of the Brown Street Bridge.

THE CONTENTIOUS SAGA OF THE MAIN STREET BRIDGE

Much of the flooding in downtown Lafayette was blamed on the constriction of river flow caused by the Main Street Bridge and Levee and the embankment of the New York Central System Railroad. As early as Saturday, March 29, talk had begun of alleviating this constriction and damage from future floods. Many said the Main Street Bridge and railroad bridge needed to be built on a larger scale to allow more water to flow freely underneath when the river rose to flood stage. An editorial appeared in the *Lafayette Daily Courier* on March 29 titled "The Lesson of Experience," and it proffered the idea that a high-arched bridgeway extending well into the Main Street Levee would be an attractive and functional structure to replace the old steel framework bridge. With this editorial, the first salvo in what would be a protracted battle over the fate of the Main Street Bridge was fired.[240]

Unlike the Brown Street Bridge, which was rendered completely useless after the loss of its two spans, the Main Street Bridge had only settled on one pier, and with repair, it could be still functional for vehicular transport across the river. Thus, the first question that stimulated fierce debate was whether or not to repair or replace the bridge. As of Saturday, March 29, the *Lafayette Morning Journal* was still reporting that the "Main Street Bridge is doomed" and that the bridge, which was slipping off its thirty-degree-tilted pier, would fall into the river "by daylight" on Sunday March 30.[241] When this dire prediction failed to come true, the repair versus replace debate continued and, in the process, delayed definitive action by the Tippecanoe County Commissioners until further studies could be done by engineers.

The Tippecanoe County Commissioners consulted with engineers from Purdue University and the civil engineer and former president of the Lafayette Bridge Company Everett B. Vawter. Vawter had been a leader on the west side during the recent flood crisis and was the current Lafayette public waterworks president and a city engineer for Lafayette. Vawter and Purdue professors Albert Smith and Robert Sackett made an initial assessment of the bridge on April 7, 1913, and made the report to the county commissioners that revealed that the soundings indicated that the piers had been undermined to a depth of ten feet by the velocity of the floodwater passing around the piers.[242] It was the opinion of the three engineers that some part of the support on which the stone pier rested had been torn loose by the flood current, causing the stone pier to tip and give the appearance that it had sunk into the riverbed or had been washed away. The final opinion of the engineers was that widening of the stone piers to accommodate the Fort Wayne and Norther Indiana Traction Company tracks had caused scouring of the riverbed, the subsequent dipping of the pier and, without intervention, would cause the bridge to collapse.[243]

With this report, the debate then shifted from the question of repairing versus replacing, to the question of what type of bridge should replace the damaged steel structure. Initially, both the *Lafayette Daily Courier* and the *Lafayette Morning Journal* agreed and promoted the idea that the bridge needed to have a "large degree of structural beauty," along with being longer, more stable and allow a greater degree of water flowage, especially during periods of high water.[244] The county commissioners on whom the decision-making responsibility was placed were facing increasing public pressure by resolutions and community petitions from Lafayette merchants, businessmen and citizens who were demanding quick decisions and concrete actions to save the faltering Lafayette businesses and restore the local economy by improving transportation across the river.[245]

While this debate gathered steam, the commissioners once again awarded a bid to Wallace Marshall's Lafayette Engineering Company to install a series of wire cables and heavy ropes to tie the sagging spans of the Main Street Bridge together and to keep the spans from slipping off of the tilted pier.[246] With the temporary stabilization of the spans, the bridge was reopened on the afternoon of April 17, but it was closed the next day, when Everett Vawter and Professor Albert Smith, both of whom had initially advised the commissioners on the state of the bridge, were joined by Purdue professor W.K. Hatt in identifying a potentially dangerous crack in the west pier.[247] The commissioners asked David Hanson, the diver who was employed by the Lake Erie and Western Railroad to inspect and repair the New York Central System Railroad Bridge, to inspect the pier on the Main Street Bridge.

Hanson inspected the bridge the next day and found that the Main Street Bridge's stone pier had been built on a wooden support structure that had been severely damaged by the floodwaters. In his opinion, the remaining wooden support was insufficient to support the pier and "may give way at any time and throw the bridge into the river."[248] The wooden structure was composed of twelve rows of wooden pilings that had been driven vertically into the riverbed, on which rested a horizontal platform, or grillage, of thick timbers. It was on this horizontal platform that the stone pier actually rested and not the riverbed itself or the bedrock below the riverbed. The diver found that the scouring effect from the stone pier's downstream eddy had caused two-thirds of the twelve rows of vertical pilings to be uprooted and washed away by the torrential flood current, leaving only four rows arranged perpendicularly to the axis of the pier. Although the horizontal grillage platform on which the pier rested was mostly intact, the four remaining rows of vertical pilings that supported the grillage platform were all near the center of the pier, making the pilings act like the fulcrum in the middle of a teeter-totter and allowing the horizontal grillage platform to tip in the downstream direction until its downstream edge came to rest on the riverbed. The upstream edge of the grillage platform was lifted about seven feet above the riverbed, providing sufficient room for the diver to walk completely under the grillage platform and look up at the underside of the tilted pier's base. The stone pier tilted at the same angle as the platform on which it rested, resulting in the downstream side of the pier submerging and creating the impression that the pier was sinking or had washed away. The bridge decking and spans supported by the pier likewise tilted at a similar angle, causing the ironwork of the rest of the bridge to twist under the forces of gravity. On receiving the report, the three engineers recommended closing the Main Street Bridge immediately to "travel of any character."[249]

The county commissioners continued to mull over the options on what to do with the Main Street Bridge throughout April. At the same time, officials of the Fort Wayne and Northern Indiana Traction Company were not content to wait for the commissioners to act on the Main Street Bridge; they had already made plans of their own to re-establish a traction rail line bridge across the river to replace the unusable tracks attached to Main Street Bridge. The traction rail company had already acquired the pilings and steel necessary to build a bridge and were waiting for the commissioners to make a decision on the Main Street Bridge before proceeding. If the commissioners were not forthcoming with a definite decision shortly, the traction company would petition for permission to build its own bridge independent of what was done with the Main Street Bridge.[250]

Two days later, on April 30, the engineers Vawter, Smith and Hatt recommended to the commissioners that no attempt should be made to restore the then-present Main Street Bridge to its former condition, as such a decision would be "unwise and uneconomical."[251] The engineers advised the county commissioners to proceed with plans for a new bridge and that the old bridge be temporarily stabilized by supporting and reinforcing false work placed under the bridge to hold it securely in place until the new bridge could be constructed. Beginning the day after this announcement, the *Lafayette Daily Courier* began running daily photographs portraying examples of beautiful arched concrete bridges tied to the editorial message that this grand design could be how the new Main Street Bridge might possibly appear given appropriate decisions made by the county commissioners.

The May 17 county commissioners meeting resulted in $12,000 being allocated to repair the Main Street Bridge, but nothing definite was decided regarding the new bridge. Three days later, the Lafayette Engineering Company was again awarded the contract to repair the old Main Street Bridge to a degree that was sufficient for safe vehicular use. For the Fort Wayne Traction Rail Company, the lack of new bridge plans meant yet another delay. The traction company couldn't finalize their own bridge plans because they had to know how the Main Street Levee was going to be altered to accommodate the new Main Street Bridge before it could place and align its new traction rail bridge with the levee.

By June 4, it appeared the commissioners were about to make significant progress by reviewing and approving one of the plans submitted by the same engineers the county had employed for advice and assessment on the Main Street Bridge: Vawter, Smith and Hatt. The new designs embraced the aesthetic smooth concrete arch style favored by the commissioners and the newspapers, with the functional argument that the wider arch design accommodated more free water flow underneath. The county engineers submitted one steel design and one concrete design to give the commissioners two options.[252] On June 6, the newspapers reported that a "concrete bridge [was] certain to be built by the county." The concrete design would be very wide, with a double set of streetcar tracks down the center, presumably for the Fort Wayne and Northern Indiana Traction Company. The cost was estimated to be $250,000, which was considerably higher than what the newspapers at the time had speculated ($70,000 to $80,000).

The traction line company appealed to the commissioners that it had already invested $20,000 on the bridge it was intending to build independently and could not afford to lose this investment by not completing the bridge. Its request for permission to complete its bridge parallel to the new Main Street Bridge was refused because its piers would not align with the piers of the proposed Main Street Bridge (hence creating problems with rivercraft navigation and increasing resistance to river flow) and because the traction line company bridge "would spoil the appearance of the new bridge."[253]

It did not take long for the traction railroad officials to reject the new Main Street Bridge plans offered by the county commissioners. The commissioners were requesting the Fort Wayne and Northern Indiana Traction Company pay a one-time cost of $40,000 for permanent rights to use the double rails across the new Main Street Bridge. The traction company's position was that it had invested $20,000 on its own bridge and would not pay any more than $20,000 to be a part of the Main Street Bridge. If it was not allowed to build its own independent bridge, the traction company said it would likely build one anyway. After several meetings between officials of the traction company and the county commissioners, on July 18, the *Lafayette Daily Courier* announced the negotiations were deadlocked, creating yet another delay.[254]

A group of prominent Lafayette businessmen, seeing that any further delay of the Main Street Bridge opening would directly affect their businesses, began independent negotiations with the county commissioners and the traction line company. With the businessmen brokering a deal, on July 23, it was announced that that the traction line company would pay $32,000 for rights to use the tracks on the new Main Street Bridge. And at the same time, it was announced that the traction line company would split the cost with the county for construction of a temporary traction line rail bridge and pedestrian walkway that would be used until the new Main Street Bridge could be completed.[255]

Specifications for the proposed new Main Street Bridge were worked out by the three county engineers, approved by the county commissioners and

In the fall of 1913, a temporary wooden walkway across the Wabash River was built next to the trusses (falsework) supporting the Main Street Bridge. A temporary traction car railway bridge was built next to the pedestrian walkway. Ice jams that winter destroyed both the temporary traction rail bridge and the wooden walkway. *Photograph courtesy of Tippecanoe County Historical Association.*

On September 12, 1913, a large steam-driven pile driver that was being used to drive wooden pilings for the temporary street railway bridge tipped over, hurtling two men twenty feet to the ground. In this rare photograph, Joseph Thompson can be seen lying on the ground on the right side of the image, and he is being attended to by two other men (*blurry*) while Kelly Ewing is hidden under the trestle by the steam from the steam boiler. Both men survived their injuries. *Photograph courtesy of Tippecanoe County Historical Association.*

then put out for bids on August 8, 1913. Within forty-eight hours of the specifications being released, the progress forward once again ground to a halt, as Wallace Marshall, the head of the Lafayette Engineering Company, which had been doing the repair work on the Brown Street and old Main Street Bridges, filed a formal protest that the specifications for the new bridge would not allow a sufficient flow of water under flood conditions, refuting the claims made by the county engineers for their bridge plans.[256]

Debate raged in the local newspapers, with the three county engineers and Marshall contending equally "rabidly" that their positions were mathematically correct. Marshall's contention was that the multiple "pigeonholes" designed into the county engineer's bridge design would quickly fill with debris during flood stages, eliminating them as areas through which water could flow. Further, the arch design meant that, at higher floodwaters, the presence of the arch would reduce the proportional amount of water that could flow under the bridge as the water crashed against the curved arches. In response, the county engineers asserted that their claims of sufficient free water flow with the longer bridge design was supported by the standard mathematical formulas used for calculating free water flow under the bridge.

Once again, with no apparent break in the contentions by either side, the *Lafayette Daily Courier* stepped in as an "umpire" by seeking out and procuring the opinion of a "disinterested engineer" of high credentials. The opinion was published in August 23, 1913, and outlined how the square-shaped or boxed-shaped opening design favored by Marshall would allow for a greater flow of water without having to raise the height of the bridge or the levee approach to the bridge as would be required with the arched bridge design.[257] The same day the report was published, Wallace Marshall filed his own plans for a boxed-opening bridge made of concrete-encased steel, a relatively new engineering approach at the time. Daniel B. Luten, a Purdue graduate and civil engineer from Indianapolis, also filed two plans of his own. Having passed the deadline for filing any further bridge plans, the commissioners had to decide between the original plans submitted by their own county engineers, the plan proposed by Marshall and the two plans submitted by Luten.[258]

As the county commissioners contemplated the plans submitted to them, the war of words continued, with Wallace Marshall claiming the local newspapers misrepresented his claims. Marshall also took the three county commissioners on a tour throughout the state to visit concrete bridges in flood-ravaged areas to show them how poorly concrete would stand up to a flood if the bridge was not properly designed for water flow. Said one commissioner about the trip, he was willing to be shown but did not expect to change his mind away from the proposal submitted by the three county engineers.[259] Editorials in both Lafayette papers continued to call for heeding expert evidence to resolve the dispute. But the predictions were that the three county commissioners would stand by "their" county engineers. The plans and specifications for the four submitted bridge designs were let for construction bids from companies interested in building the bridge from one or more of the submitted designs. The deadline for the submission of construction bids was September 3, and on the appointed date, the sealed bids were opened, and the county commissioners turned the bids over to the county engineers for review.[260] Three days later, and to the surprise of many, the vote was two commissioners to one in favor of the Marshall boxed-opening design bridge plan to be constructed by Marshall's Lafayette

The Main Street Bridge's construction during the winter of 1913–14. After a lot of controversy about materials and design, the final design called for huge steel beams encased in concrete. Although the squared appearance of the bridge design was less esthetically pleasing than an arched design, the Wallace Marshall design was considered superior in strength and water flowage during high-water conditions. *From the postcard collection of Arnold L. Sweet.*

The Main Street Bridge, circa 1925. The eventual design of the Main Street Bridge reflected the priority given to increasing the water flow space beneath the bridge during high flood stages. The Main Street Bridge remained open for traffic until 1996, when it was converted into a pedestrian bridge. It is still used today. *From the postcard collection of Arnold L. Sweet.*

Engineering Company. The one commissioner who asserted he would not change his mind from supporting the original county engineers' plan held true to his claim and was the lone dissenting vote.[261] So, eight and a half months after the Main Street Bridge was damaged by the flood, the county commissioners finally had a plan and a builder selected to replace the old bridge with a next generation bridge.

Work began in late September 1913, and in spite of some setbacks over the winter due to ice jams damaging the supporting falsework and destroying the temporary traction line bridge and walkway that had been put up parallel to the bridge, in July 1914, the new Main Street Bridge finally opened.

Like the Brown Street Bridge, the Main Street Bridge weathered floods and ice jams for the next eight decades. However, in 1996, its aging condition, concerns about its ability to handle heavy traffic and the opportunity for redesigning downtown Lafayette traffic patterns with the massive railroad relocation project marked the end of the 1914 Main Street Bridge for vehicular traffic. However, the bridge was retrofitted with lights and a new walking surface and converted into the John T. Myers Pedestrian Bridge, a popular highlight of the downtown Lafayette riverfront.

COULD THIS FLOODING HAPPEN AGAIN?

In the days following the Great Flood of 1913, communities throughout the Midwest asked the question: "Can this flooding happen again?" The increased source of river water for the 1913 flood resulted almost entirely from five inches of rain over a few days. How this relatively small amount of rain could have resulted in a flood level of thirty-three feet in Tippecanoe County and a flowrate that exceeded that of Niagara Falls seems incongruous. Unlike previous floods, where a heavy snowpack suddenly melted, no such snowpack existed prior to the 1913 flood. However, the warm temperatures had melted what snow had fallen in the days before Easter, and the ground in the Midwest was largely saturated, preventing the new rainfall from soaking into the ground. Instead, the rain flowed directly into the streams and rivers.[262]

Still, the extensive amount of flood damage in Tippecanoe County was traced back to man-made intrusions on the natural river flow through the community. Flood banks and other barriers to high water were not typically put in place in the late nineteenth and early twentieth centuries, as floods were considered something that affected the "flood plains";

therefore, any buildings or infrastructure constructed in such an area were considered to be short-sighted and foolish. However, in the case of the 1913 flood, industry was expanding, and as the memory of previous floods faded, demand for more buildings, factories to accommodate the burgeoning industry, meant structures were built in these potential flood areas, as evidenced by the buildings lost in the Chauncey Bottomlands and the basin between the Main Street and Brown Street Levees. In retrospect, the failure to erect high banks on the west side of the river allowed the rising river current to easily breech the low banks, filling the lowlands with flood currents that were then unable to continue to flow downstream because of the encroachment of the man-made Main Street Levee and the railroad embankment. Indeed, while reflecting on a similar situation in Indianapolis, the *Indianapolis Star* placed the blame for the 1913 flood destruction of downtown Indianapolis squarely on the encroachment of the "natural bed of the White River" by man-made structures that limited the volume that could flow safely through the community.[263]

Since 1913, both sides of the Wabash Riverbanks in the Lafayette area have been raised, and the lowland between Main Street and Brown Street and between Main Street and the railroad embankment have been filled with earth, elevating all structures in these previous bottomlands. Although, today, certain low areas along the Wabash River in Tippecanoe County still flood almost every year, their locations are well known (e.g., North River Road just north of West Lafayette and the State Road 225 approach to the Jewettsport Ford Bridge at Battleground) and contain no significant development. Greater zoning regulations and limitations on the ability to obtain flood insurance help ensure that businesses, housing or infrastructure will be built above the demarcation of the one-hundred-year floodplain. Still, as history has repeatedly shown, man-made structures built to contain or guard against the full wrath of nature and weather are seldom successful. It is through remembering historical events such as the 1913 flood in Tippecanoe County that future safeguards can be taken to reduce the impact of such catastrophic events on our communities in the future.

NOTES

Introduction

1. Smithsonian Institution Archives online, "Postcard History," www.siarchives.si.edu.

Chapter 1

2. R.C. Kriebel, "William Digby (1802–1864)," in *Old Lafayette 1811–1853* (Lafayette, IN: Tippecanoe County Historical Association, 1988), 79.
3. Visit Lafayette (West Lafayette website), www.homeofpurdue.com.
4. R.P. DeHart, ed., *Past and Present of Tippecanoe County, Indiana* (Indianapolis: B.F. Bowen & Company, 1909), 1:374.
5. Ibid., 1:423.
6. "Improvement and Contracting News," *Paving and Mechanical Engineering* 5, no. 1 (July 1893): 198; DeHart, *Past and Present*, 1:463–64.
7. L. Esarey, *History of Indiana* (Washington, D.C.: National Historical Association Inc., 1928), 79.
8. DeHart, *Past and Present*, 1:428–29.
9. Ibid., 1:429–30.
10. Ibid., 1:429.
11. Bob Kriebel, "Mark Twain Visited, Poked Fun at Lafayette in 1885," *Lafayette Journal and Courier*, July 11, 2010, 8.

12. DeHart, "History of Transportation in Tippecanoe County, Indiana," in *Past and Present*, 1:372.
13. H.R. Grant, *Follow the Flag: The History of the Wabash Railroad* (DeKalb: Northern Illinois University Press, 2004), 111, 251.
14. Historic Indianapolis, "uniontractionmap.1913.utexas," www.historicindianapolis.com; G.A. Blackburn, "Interurban Railroads of Indiana," *Indiana Magazine of History* 20, no. 3 (September 1924): 221–79.
15. R.L. Sackett, "The Wabash River Flood of 1913, at Lafayette, Ind.," in *Proceedings of the Indiana Academy of Science* (Indianapolis: Wm.B.Burford Contractor for State Printing and Binding, 1913), 23:64.
16. Ibid., 65.

Chapter 2

17. Henry J. Cox, ed., "Report for January 1913," *The Report of the US Department of Agriculture Weather Bureau, Climatological Service District No. 4, The Lake Region*, 1913.
18. "Terrific Gale Causes Loss of Life and Great Property Damage," *Lafayette Daily Courier*, March 21, 1913, 1.
19. "Henry Walter Is Killed by Falling Fosters Store Sign," *Lafayette Daily Courier*, March 21, 1913, 1.
20. "Terrific Gale," *Lafayette Daily Courier*, 1.
21. Ibid., 6; "More Storm Damage," *Lafayette Daily Courier*, March 22, 1913, 3.
22. "Terrific Gale," *Lafayette Daily Courier*, 6.
23. Ibid.
24. Ibid.
25. Ibid.
26. Ibid.
27. Ibid.
28. Ibid.
29. "Damage," *Lafayette Daily Courier*, 3.
30. "Terrific Gale," *Lafayette Daily Courier*, 1.
31. "Weather Indications," *Lafayette Daily Courier*, March 22, 1913, 12.
32. "Fine Easter Predicted," *Lafayette Daily Courier*, March 22, 1913, 8.
33. "Indiana Suffers Loss of Life and Property in Gale," *Lafayette Morning Journal*, March 22, 1913, 1.
34. "Relief Rushed to Needy Storm Victims, Wire Service Badly Crippled," *Lafayette Daily Courier*, March 22, 1913, 2.

35. "Indiana Suffers," *Lafayette Morning Journal*, 1.
36. "Leaves Ruin in Wake, The Dead," *Lafayette Morning Journal*, March 22, 1913, 1.
37. Midwest Regional Climate Center, "The Great Flood of 1913 100 Years Later," www.mrcc.illinois.edu.
38. Ibid.
39. Ibid.
40. Ibid.
41. National Weather Service, "Easter Came Early in 1913 Omaha Tornado," National Oceanic and Atmospheric Administration, www.weather.gov.
42. Geoff Williams, *Washed Away* (New York: Pegasus Books, 2013), 10.
43. Ibid.; Nebraska Library Commission, "100 Years Ago This Month: The Omaha Easter Tornado of 1913," www.nlcblogs.nebraska.gov; "Continue Searching for the Living and the Dead," *Lincoln Daily Star*, March 25, 1913, 1.
44. Williams, *Away*, 9.
45. Mike Tobias, "Devil Clouds: Tornadoes Strike Nebraska—A Look Back at the 1913 Easter Sunday Tornadoes," NET News, www.netnebraska.org.
46. Nebraska Library Commission, "100 Years Ago."
47. Williams, *Away*, 24.
48. Ibid., 23.
49. National Weather Service, "Easter Came Early."

Chapter 3

50. "Easter Weather," *Lafayette Daily Courier*, March 24, 1913, 1.
51. "River Far Out of Banks," *Lafayette Daily Courier*, March 24, 1913, 1.
52. Midwest Regional Climate Center, "The Great Flood of 1913 100 Years Later," www.mrcc.illinois.edu.
53. "Another Flood Victim," *Lafayette Morning Journal*, March 25, 1913, 3.
54. "Four Lives Lost by Drowning in Raging Waters," *Indianapolis Star*, March 25, 1913, 1, www.newspapers.com.
55. "Boat Overturns and Two Men Lose Lives," *Lafayette Daily Courier*, March 25, 1913, 3.
56. "Elva Myers Clung to Tree While His Companions Died," *Lafayette Morning Journal*, March 25, 1913, 1, 3.
57. "Boat Overturns," *Lafayette Daily Courier*, 3.

58. "Elva Myers," *Lafayette Morning Journal*, 1, 3.
59. Ibid.
60. Ibid.
61. Ibid.
62. Ibid.
63. "Far Out," *Lafayette Daily Courier*, 1.
64. Ibid.
65. Ibid.
66. "Terrific Surge of Water Crumbles Steel Structure," *Lafayette Daily Courier*, March 25, 1913, 1; "River Rising at Alarming Rate," *Lafayette Morning Journal*, March 25, 1913, 3.
67. "Far Out," *Lafayette Daily Courier*, 1.

Chapter 4

68. Sackett, "Wabash River," 63–68.
69. "Terrific Surge," *Lafayette Daily Courier*, 1.
70. Ibid., 7.
71. "Lafayette Faces Worst Flood in Thirty Years," *Lafayette Morning Journal*, March 26, 1913, 2, 4.
72. Ibid.
73. Sackett, "Wabash River," 65.
74. "Terrific Surge," *Lafayette Daily Courier*, 7; "Worst Flood," *Lafayette Morning Journal*, 1.
75. Ibid.
76. Sackett, "Wabash River," figure 2, 67.
77. "Worst Flood," *Lafayette Morning Journal*, 1.
78. Ibid.
79. Ibid.
80. "Recover Body of Leland Woolery, Funeral to be Held Monday," *Purdue Exponent*, April 6, 1913, 3.
81. "Student Drowned as He Attempts to Affect a Rescue," *Lafayette Daily Courier*, March 25, 1913, 1; "Worst Flood," *Lafayette Morning Journal*, 1–2.
82. Ibid., 2.
83. "Student Drowned," *Lafayette Daily Courier*, 1.
84. "Worst Flood," *Lafayette Morning Journal*, 2; "West Lafayette is Getting Over Fright," *Lafayette Daily Courier*, March 28, 1913, 5.
85. "Worst Flood," *Lafayette Morning Journal*, 8.

86. Sackett, "Wabash River," 67.
87. "Terrific Surge," *Lafayette Daily Courier*, 1.
88. "Main Street Being Swept Away," *Lafayette Daily Courier*, March 26, 1913, 1.
89. "Isolated," *Lafayette Daily Courier*, 2.
90. "Main Street," *Lafayette Daily Courier*, 1; "Worst Flood," *Lafayette Morning Journal*, 2.
91. "Traction Bridge Goes," *Lafayette Morning Journal*, March 26, 1913, 9; "Wildcat Bridge Damaged," *Lafayette Daily Courier*, March 25, 1913, 1.
92. "Goes," *Lafayette Morning Journal*, 9.
93. "Worst Flood," *Lafayette Morning Journal*, 2.
94. Fred D. Cavinder, *The Indiana Book of Records, Firsts, and Fascinating Facts* (Bloomington: Indiana University Press, 1985), 12.
95. "Terrific Surge," *Lafayette Daily Courier*, 7; "Worst Flood," *Lafayette Morning Journal*, 2.
96. *Public Health Survey of Lafayette Indiana and Tippecanoe County, Part 1* (N.p.: Murray Philip Horwood, 1921), 8–10; "Terrific Surge," *Lafayette Daily Courier*, 7.
97. "Will Remodel Power House," *Electric Traction Weekly* 4, no. 49 (December 5, 1908): 1,295; "Power House and Substations," *Electric Railway Review* 17, no. 1 (January 5, 1907): 27; "Current Electrical News," *Electrical Review* 45, no. 23 (December 3, 1904): 941.
98. "Power House Is Fighting for Life," *Lafayette Morning Journal*, March 26, 1913, 2.
99. "Lafayette Gas Plant Forced to Stop Its Engines," *Lafayette Morning Journal*, March 26, 1913, 9.
100. "Ice Company Vacates Barns," *Lafayette Morning Journal*, March 26, 1913, 9.
101. "Worst Flood," *Lafayette Morning Journal*, 8.

Chapter 5

102. Ibid., 2.
103. "Main Street Bridge Is Now Being Rapidly Swept Away," *Lafayette Daily Courier*, March 26, 1913, 1.
104. W.R. Cade, "Flood on the Wabash River 1913; in The Floods of 1913 in the Rivers of the Ohio and Lower Mississippi Valleys," bulletin Z, Alfred J. Henry, U.S. Department of Agriculture, Weather Bureau, December 31, 1913, 75.

105. "City Is Isolated," *Lafayette Daily Courier*, March 23, 1913, 1.
106. "Scores Reported Killed When Dam Breaks at Dayton," *Lafayette Morning Journal*, March 23, 1913, 1.
107. "Other Bridges in Danger," *Lafayette Morning Journal*, March 26, 1913, 2.
108. "Worst Flood," *Lafayette Morning Journal*, 87.
109. Ibid., 2; "West Side Suffers in Flood's Grip," *Lafayette Morning Journal*, March 27, 1913, 1.
110. "Street Cars Stopped," *Lafayette Morning Journal*, March 27, 1913, 1.
111. Ibid.
112. "Main Street Bridge Broken," *Lafayette Morning Journal*, March 27, 1913, 3.
113. "Mayor Issues Warning Proclamation to People," *Lafayette Daily Courier*, March 26, 1913, 1.
114. "Firemen Made Brave Fight," *Lafayette Morning Journal*, March 27, 1913, 1, 3.
115. "Bought a Tank of Oil at Brookston," *Lafayette Morning Journal*, March 27, 1913, 3.
116. "West Side," *Lafayette Morning Journal*, 1.
117. Ibid.
118. "Monon Shops Closed," *Lafayette Morning Journal*, March 27, 1913, 1.
119. "Bought a Tank," *Lafayette Morning Journal*, 3.
120. "West Side," *Lafayette Morning Journal*, 1.
121. "Miscellany of Flood," *Lafayette Daily Courier*, March 27, 1913, 1.
122. "Circus Property Lost," *Lafayette Morning Journal*, March 27, 1913, 1.
123. "Police Effect Rescue," *Lafayette Daily Courier*, March 26, 1913, 1.
124. "Dashed to Pieces Against Bridge," *Lafayette Morning Journal*, March 27, 1913, 1.
125. Ibid.
126. "Dr. Whitesell Is Very Much Alive," *Lafayette Morning Journal*, March 27, 1913, 3.
127. "Dog Escaped Flood," *Lafayette Daily Courier*, April 1, 1913, 6.
128. "Announcement," *Lafayette Morning Journal*, March 29, 1913, 6.
129. "Water Supply Has Been Exhausted," *Lafayette Morning Journal*, March 27, 1913, 1.
130. "Today's Journal Set Largely by Hand," *Lafayette Morning Journal*, March 27, 1913, 3.
131. "Courier Set by Hand," *Lafayette Daily Courier*, March 27, 1913, 6.
132. "West Lafayette Has Food Supply for Several Days," *Lafayette Morning Journal*, March 28, 1913, 3.

Chapter 6

133. "River Gauges Show Rate of River Fall," *Lafayette Daily Courier*, March 27, 1913, 1.
134. "West Lafayette," *Lafayette Morning Journal*, 1.
135. "River Gauges," *Lafayette Daily Courier*, 1.
136. "Hero Beats Flood," *Lafayette Daily Courier*, March 27, 1913, 1.
137. "Railroad Bridge Safe," *Lafayette Daily Courier*, March 27, 1913, 1.
138. Ibid.
139. "Safe," *Lafayette Daily Courier*, 6.
140. *Document of the General Assembly of Indiana at the 43rd Regular Session Begun on the 8th Day of January 1863, Volume 1, Part 2* (Indianapolis: Joseph J. Bingham, 1863), 818, www.books.google.com; "Monon Bridge Standing," *Lafayette Morning Journal*, March 28, 1913, 1.
141. "Lake Erie Train Here from East," *Lafayette Morning Journal*, March 28, 1913, 3.
142. "Standing," *Lafayette Morning Journal*, 1.
143. "Flood at Dayton Subsiding Fast," *Lafayette Morning Journal*, March 28, 1913, 1.
144. "West Side Conditions Are Now Improving," *Lafayette Daily Courier*, March 27, 1913, 3.
145. "Four Horse Team," *Lafayette Morning Journal*, March 28, 1913, 1.
146. "Club Houses Still Safe," *Lafayette Daily Courier*, March 28, 1913, 1.
147. "No Promise of Gas," *Lafayette Daily Courier*, March 27, 1913, 10.
148. "Gas Notice," *Lafayette Morning Journal*, March 28, 1913, 1.
149. "West Lafayette," *Lafayette Morning Journal*, 1.
150. "Notice," *Lafayette Morning Journal*, 1.
151. "Martin Clock Still Ticking," *Lafayette Morning Journal*, March 29, 1913, 2.
152. "Now Improving," *Lafayette Daily Courier*, 3.
153. Ibid.
154. "No Show at Dryfus," *Lafayette Daily Courier*, March 27, 1913, 6.
155. J. Duplaga and S. Fletcher, "Historic Theater Case Study—Lafayette Theater," Indiana Department of Natural Resources, Historic Preservation and Archeology, www.in.gov.
156. "Family Theater," *Lafayette Daily Courier*, March 27, 1913, 8.
157. "Indiana Craft Brewpub's Revival Sparked by Prohibition History," *Lafayette Journal and Courier*, August 19, 2016, www.jconline.com.
158. "One Factory Still Open," *Lafayette Daily Courier*, March 27, 1913, 8.

159. "River Is Falling Little Each Hour and Hope Reigns," *Lafayette Morning Journal*, March 28, 1913, 1.
160. Ibid.
161. "Celina Reservoir Declared Safe," *Lafayette Daily Courier*, March 28, 1913, 1.
162. "Hope Reigns," *Lafayette Morning Journal*, 1.
163. "Busy Page," *Lafayette Morning Journal*, March 28, 1913, 1.
164. "Phone Service Restored," *Lafayette Daily Courier*, March 28, 1913, 1.
165. "Talking Lines to West Lafayette," *Lafayette Morning Journal*, March 28, 1913, 3.
166. "Water Works Pumps Will Start Today," *Lafayette Morning Journal*, March 28, 1913, 2.
167. "Clarence Jamison Gets Back Home," *Lafayette Morning Journal*, March 28, 1913, 3.
168. "False Alarm," *Lafayette Morning Journal*, March 28, 1913, 3.
169. "Aronzon Dashed into Fragments," *Lafayette Morning Journal*, March 28, 1913, 3.
170. Ibid.
171. "Club Houses," *Lafayette Daily Courier*, 1.

Chapter 7

172. "River Falling Fast and City's Isolation Is Thing of the Past," *Lafayette Daily Courier*, March 28, 1913, 1.
173. Midwest Regional Climate Center at University of Illinois, "The Great Flood of 1913, Community Profiles: Lafayette, Indiana," www.mrcc.illinois.edu.
174. "Gas on To-Night," *Lafayette Daily Courier*, March 28, 1913, 1.
175. "Lafayette Recovering from Flood but Damage Done Here Is Very Extensive," *Lafayette Daily Courier*, March 29, 1913, 1.
176. "Fake News," *Lafayette Morning Journal*, March 31, 1913, 5.
177. "The Bridge Question," *Lafayette Morning Journal*, March 31, 1913, 5.
178. "The Lesson of Experience," *Lafayette Daily Courier*, March 29, 1913, 4; "Question," *Lafayette Morning Journal*, 5.
179. "Lesson," *Lafayette Daily Courier*, 4; "Question," *Lafayette Morning Journal*, 5.
180. Ibid.
181. "Lafayette Recovering," *Lafayette Daily Courier*, 1; "Levee Presents a Strange Sight," *Lafayette Morning Journal*, March 29, 1913, 1.

182. "One Gas Machine Is Working Now," *Lafayette Morning Journal*, March 29, 1913, 1.
183. "Lafayette Recovering," *Lafayette Daily Courier*, 1; "Gas Turned On," *Lafayette Morning Journal*, March 31, 1913, 1.
184. "Lafayette Recovering," *Lafayette Daily Courier*, 1.
185. "Street Lights Are Turned on Again," *Lafayette Morning Journal*, March 31, 1913, 2.
186. "Fires Started Under Boilers," *Lafayette Morning Journal*, March 28, 1913, 1.
187. "Pumping Station Safe," *Lafayette Daily Courier*, March 29, 1913, 2.
188. "Water Supply Gone: Fire Danger Great," *Lafayette Daily Courier*, March 28, 1913, 1.
189. "Big Pump Forcing Water into Mains," *Lafayette Morning Journal*, March 29, 1913, 1.
190. "Supply Gone," *Lafayette Daily Courier*, 1.
191. "Traction Line Is Ready to Operate," *Lafayette Morning Journal*, March 29, 1913, 3.
192. "Lafayette Recovering," *Lafayette Daily Courier*, 1; "Warning to All Health Officers and the People of Indiana," *Lafayette Daily Courier*, March 29, 1913, 8.
193. "Public Health Notice," *Lafayette Daily Courier*, March 29, 1913, 5.
194. "Big Pump," *Lafayette Morning Journal*, 1.
195. "Will Continue Shuttle Service," *Lafayette Morning Journal*, March 31, 1913, 7; "River Is Falling Little Each Hour and Hope Returns," *Lafayette Morning Journal*, March 28, 1913, 1.
196. Ibid.
197. "Personal and General," *Lafayette Daily Courier*, March 29, 1913, 2.
198. "Hope Returns," *Lafayette Morning Journal*, 7.
199. Ibid.
200. "Supt. Hight Announced Resumption of Classes Monday," *Lafayette Daily Courier*, March 29, 1913, 2.
201. "Lafayette Recovering," *Lafayette Daily Courier*, 1.
202. Advertisement, *Lafayette Daily Courier*, March 29, 1913, 8.
203. "City and West Side Water Is Pure," *Lafayette Daily Courier*, April 3, 1913, 1.
204. "Watch the Water Supply," *Lafayette Daily Courier*, April 3, 1913, 4.
205. "Notice to Everybody Who Had Goods Damaged by Water," *Lafayette Daily Courier*, April 2, 1913, 10.
206. "Search for Bodies," *Lafayette Daily Courier*, March 28, 1913, 1.

207. "Bodies Not Found," *Lafayette Daily Courier*, April 3, 1913, 5.
208. "Body Is Recovered," *South Bend Tribune*, April 8, 1913, 4.
209. "Hundreds Search for Body," *Times* (Munster, IN), April 29, 1913, 6.
210. "Drowned Student's Father Arrives Here," *Lafayette Daily Courier*, March 28, 1913, 1.
211. "Drowned Student's Body Is Recovered," *Lafayette Daily Courier*, April 5, 1913, 6.
212. "Recover Body," *Purdue University Exponent*, 3.
213. "Usual Services in Commemoration of Purdue's Dead," *Purdue University Exponent*, May 29, 1913, 1.
214. "Hope Reigns," *Lafayette Morning Journal*, 1.
215. "Ferry Boat Will Be Launched Tomorrow," *Lafayette Daily Courier*, April 1, 1913, 1.
216. "Ferry Line Will Be Opened Next Week," *Lafayette Daily Courier*, April 2, 1913, 1.
217. Ibid.
218. "Boats Only Means of Crossing Wabash," *Lafayette Daily Courier*, April 3, 1913, 1.
219. "Another Ferry," *Lafayette Morning Journal*, March 29, 1913, 6.
220. "Opened Next Week," *Lafayette Daily Courier*, 1.
221. "Ferry and Cars to Give Good Service Across the River," *Lafayette Daily Courier*, April 4, 1913, 1.
222. "Ferry Is Stalled Again," *Lafayette Daily Courier*, April 9, 1913, 1.
223. Ibid.
224. "Will Have Pontoon Bridge," *Indianapolis Star*, April 11, 1913, 1.
225. "Fight on to Save Main Street Bridge," *Lafayette Daily Courier*, April 14, 1913, 4.
226. "Crowd Seizes the Ferry," *Lafayette Daily Courier*, April 17, 1913, 5.
227. "With Bridges Down Trade Is Suffering," *Lafayette Daily Courier*, April 9, 1913, 6.
228. "Good Service," *Lafayette Daily Courier*, 1.
229. "Opening of Bridge," *Lafayette Daily Courier*, April 18, 1913, 1.
230. "Lake Erie Bridge Open," *Lafayette Daily Courier*, April 18, 1913, 1.
231. "Bridge Being Used," *Lafayette Daily Courier*, April 28, 1913, 8.
232. "Brown Street Bridge Will Have a New Span," *Lafayette Daily Courier*, July 9, 1913, 1.
233. "New Bridge Nearly Done," *Lafayette Daily Courier*, September 24, 1913, 9.
234. "Bridge to Be Closed," *Lafayette Daily Courier*, October 15, 1913, 12.
235. "Busy on Brown Street," *Lafayette Daily Courier*, November 21, 1913, 1.

236. "Brown Street Bridge Closed," *Lafayette Journal and Courier*, June 11, 1958, 1.
237. "12 Foot Crack Closes Brown Street Bridge," *Lafayette Journal and Courier*, July 4, 1973, 2.
238. "Bridge Crack Forms," *Lafayette Journal and Courier*, July 5, 1974, 3.
239. "Brown Street Bridge Being Demolished," *Lafayette Journal and Courier*, October 19, 1974, 1.
240. "Lafayette Recovering," *Lafayette Daily Courier*, 1.
241. "Lafayette Fast Recovering from Effects of Flood," *Lafayette Morning Journal*, March 29, 1913, 1.
242. "Say Bridge Is Doomed," *Lafayette Daily Courier*, April 8, 1913, 1.
243. Ibid.; "Lafayette Recovering," *Lafayette Daily Courier*, 1.
244. "A Bigger, Better, More Beautiful Bridge," *Lafayette Daily Courier*, April 10, 1913, 4.
245. "Merchants Asking Relief," *Lafayette Daily Courier*, April 10, 1913, 8.
246. "Fight," *Lafayette Daily Courier*, 4.
247. "Bridge Shut Again; Diver to Inspect," *Lafayette Daily Courier*, April 18, 1913, 1.
248. "Diver Finds Bridge Weak," *Lafayette Daily Courier*, April 21, 1913, 4.
249. Ibid.
250. "New Street Car Bridge," *Lafayette Daily Courier*, April 28, 1913, 7.
251. "Engineers Report in Favor of New Main Street Bridge," *Lafayette Daily Courier*, April 30, 1913, 1.
252. "Council May Provide for Fine New Bridge," *Lafayette Daily Courier*, June 4, 1913, 1.
253. "Concrete Bridge Is Now Certain to Be Built by the County," *Lafayette Daily Courier*, June 6, 1913, 1.
254. "Traction Officials Reject Bridge Plans," *Lafayette Daily Courier*, June 18, 1913, 8.
255. "Street Cars Soon to Cross Wabash River," *Lafayette Daily Courier*, July 23, 1913, 5.
256. "Dispute Over Bridge Plans Precipitated," *Lafayette Daily Courier*, August 11, 1913, 1.
257. "New Bridge Plans Do Not Provide Enough River Room Says Disinterested Engineer," *Lafayette Daily Courier*, August 23, 1913, 1.
258. "New Bridge Plans Filed," *Lafayette Daily Courier*, August 23, 1913, 1.
259. "Main Street Bridge Contract to be Let," *Lafayette Daily Courier*, August 30, 1913, 1.
260. "Four Companies Submit Bridge Bids; Contract Soon to Be Let," *Lafayette Daily Courier*, September 3, 1913, 1.

261. "Local Concern Will Erect New Bridge on Marshall Plans," *Lafayette Daily Courier*, September 6, 1913, 1.
262. "Cause of the Flood," *Lafayette Daily Courier*, April 2, 1913, 6.
263. Ibid.

INDEX

K

L

Y

ABOUT THE AUTHORS

Dr. Pete Bill is a retired professor from the Purdue University College of Veterinary Medicine and an amateur historian of Tippecanoe County and Purdue University history. He has amassed an extensive collection of rare and unusual artifacts from the local community, which he shares with the local historical association and the Purdue University archives. He frequently lectures on topics related to interesting historical characters and events related to Tippecanoe County, including portrayals of the local Pulitzer Prize–winning illustrator John T. McCutcheon. Dr. Bill currently serves as president of the board of the Tippecanoe County Historical Association.

Dr. Arnold Sweet is a retired professor from the Purdue University School of Industrial Engineering. He and his family moved to West Lafayette, Indiana, in 1960, when he received a Ford Foundation Fellowship that enabled him to start working on his doctorate degree. He had always been a "collector," and he started to collect postcards from Tippecanoe County. He joined the Indianapolis Postcard Club in 1975, and they have greatly helped him in growing his collection. He has given lectures using his collection at meetings of the Wabash Area Lifetime Learning Association. He is a member of the Tippecanoe County Historical Association. He also volunteers at book sales at the Tippecanoe Library in Lafayette.